Restructuring
Pakistan
A Global Imperative

Restructuring
Pakistan

A Global Imperative

Major General Vinod Saighal

Manas Publications
New Delhi-110 002 (INDIA)

MANAS PUBLICATIONS
(Publishers, Distributors, Importers & Exporters)
4819, Varun House, Mathur Lane,
24, Ansari Road, Darya Ganj,
New Delhi - 110 002 (INDIA)
Ph.: 3260783, 3265523
Fax: 011 - 3272766
E-mail: manaspublications@vsnl.com

© Vinod Saighal

First Published 2002

ISBN 81-7049-134-7

No part of this publication can be reproduced, photocopied, translated, etc. in any form whatsoever, without prior written permission of the publisher.

The views expressed in this book are those of the author and not necessarily of the publisher. The publisher is not responsible for the views of the author and authenticity of the data, in any way whatsoever.

Typeset at
Manas Publications

Printed in India at
R.K. Offset, Delhi
and Published by Mrs. Suman Lata for
Manas Publications, 4819/XI, Varun House,
Mathur Lane, 24, Ansari Road, Daryaganj
New Delhi 110002 (INDIA)

Dedication

This book is dedicated to the people of the sub-continent in the fervent hope that this troubled, seething mass of humanity finds peace – first in their own hearts and hearths, and then in their shared destiny that must manifest itself once the fires of hatred have burned themselves out from Colombo to Kabul.

Preface

Were an average, educated and aware citizen of Pakistan to be asked to sum up the genesis of the current turmoil on the globe in just one sentence he would not be far wrong were he to attribute it to the 'strategic overreach' attempted by some Pakistani generals after the Soviet pullout from Afghanistan. When examined closely it will be found that the inordinate suffering visited upon the people of Afghanistan in the last decade, linked to the spread of Islamic *jehad* and global terrorism, can be laid at the door of the ambitions of the Pakistan military to be the new masters of the Great Game, regardless of the price that Pakistan itself might have to pay for such folly.

In a manner of speaking it could be said that the situation beckoned. America had lost interest in the region after the Soviet pull back. The Soviet Union itself had collapsed. China was feeling hemmed in after the global opprobrium brought on by the *Tiananmen* Square massacre. India was on the verge of bankruptcy. It had to fly out nearly 240 tons of gold and pledge it with the Bank of England for obtaining much needed financial bail out. In Pakistan itself, after a prolonged military spell, the political parties were more interested in the internal affairs of the country. Military adventurism beckoned.

Temporarily deprived of their active governance role after the restoration of post-Zia democratic governments, the military top brass had nothing better to do than to start looking for strategic depth in Afghanistan. They were not to know at that time that their strategic misadventure could turn into a strategic nightmare that would threaten the very existence of Pakistan. By the turn of the century both the fundamentals of Pakistan - state policy and Islam - had been turned on their head. The book, *Restructuring Pakistan* attempts to chart out a route for the return of Pakistan to democracy, stability and a useful role as a dynamic member of the comity of nations and not as a surrogate for the geo-strategic machinations in the region of one or the other global power.

For much too long the destinies of countries in Asia have been fashioned by forces unleashed by the West. Whatever the other ills, one of the more promising developments in today's world has been the growth of democracies. The countries of Asia where Islam predominates must come to terms with the new global realities. Religion must be firmly pushed back where it belongs – in the confines of the human heart and within the four walls of the mosque. Its attempts to intrude into the political arena could end up by destroying the very basis of Islam. Islam cannot be destroyed from without. It will simply wither on the vine if the fresh breezes that waft from all points of the globe are not allowed to interact with it to find their own natural adjustments in the Islamic milieu. In the Cold War era the US backed dictators who smothered the democratic urge of their people. The Americans were fighting an ideology, Communism. They tried to fight it in the Islamic world through an appeal to religion: a blunder that could haunt both America and the Islamic world for a long time to come. Communism declined not due so much to the economic might or military superiority of the other superpower, but because of the declining vigour of an ideology that had run its course. It is being kept artificially alive in China and few other countries. The tragedy of communism must not be revisited on Islam in the 21st century. In country after another, by suppressing the democratic urges of the people, the autocratic regimes – mostly military – are leaving the mosque and the Muslim clergy as the only channels of protest for the ordinary person. A deadlier peril awaits these countries if they do not change course. The people of Pakistan have a historic opportunity to change tack.

Vinod Saighal

List of Acronyms

ABM	Anti Ballistic Missile (Treaty entered into between USSR and USA in 1972)
BCCI	Bank of Credit & Commerce International
CAR	Central Asian Republics
CBM	Confidence Building Measures
CIA	Central Intelligence Agency (USA)
CTBT	Comprehensive Test Ban Treaty
ECCM	Electronic Counter Counter Measures
ECM	Electronic Counter Measures
GDP	Gross Domestic Product
ISI	Inter - Services Intelligence (Directorate of Pakistan)
LOC	Line of Control (in Jammu & Kashmir between Pakistan & India)
MQM	Muhajir Qaumi Muteheda (commonly referred to as Mohajir Qaumi Movement)
NGO	Non Governmental Organisation
NMD	National Missile Defence
NWFP	North West Frontier Province (of Pakistan)
OIC	Organisation of Islamic Conference
OPEC	Organisation of Petroleum Exporting Countries
RMA	Revolution in Military Affairs
SAVAK	(Iranian Intelligence Agency of Iran during the rule of the Shah)
TMD	Theatre Missile Defence

UNEF	United Nations Emergency Force
USAF	United States Air Force
WHO	World Health Organisation
WMD	Weapons of Mass Destruction
WTC	World Trade Centre
WTO	World Trade Organisation

Contents

Dedication	5
Preface	6
List of Acronyms	9

PART-I

1.	Introduction	15
2.	Islam in a Cul de Sac	19
3.	Deconstruction of the Pakistan State	47
4.	Reconstruction	75

PART-II

5.	The Way Forward	87
6.	The New Uncertainties	107

    a. Pakistan
    b. Ghettoisation of Pakistan
    c. Afghanistan
    d. Albion At It Once Again
    e. Central Asia
    f. Iran
    g. Middle East
    h. Turkey
    i. Egypt
    j. Saudi Arabia
    k. Jordan, Syria, Israel, Lebanon
    l. Russia
    m. USA: Carpet Baggers to Carpet Bombers
    n. The Increasing Planetary Stresses
    o. Indo-Afghan

7. September 11 Events: Global Perspective 163
   a. Reformulating the Ground Rules for
      Combating Global Terrorism
   b. Islam Linked to Terror
   c. Subcontinental Fallout
   d. China
   e. The (Propagandistic) Apotheosis of the Taliban

8. Analysing the Military Strategy of the Intervention 185
   Forces
9. Random Press Samplings (Pakistan) 203
10. Epilogue (as Prologue): Dealing with 205
    the Afghan-Pak Cauldron- The Global Perspective

End Notes 229
Maps 231
Index 233

PART - I

What Went Before

1
Introduction

At the very outset the need arises to pose the basic question as to why Pakistan should be restructured. The short answer to this question that is no longer rhetorical can be given as follows:

- To prevent the *talibanisation* of Pakistan.
- To prevent a civil war breaking out in Pakistan.
- To prevent the further spread of state sponsored terrorism from the Afghanistan – Pakistan region.
- To prevent the spread of nuclear materials from this region.
- To prevent the spread of regressive Islam on the subcontinent through repression and terror.

Again, at the beginning, it has to be clarified that while India remains at the receiving end of much of the terror emanating from Pakistan it has the geographic mass, the demographic mass, the military might, the economic strength (comparatively) and the resilience to withstand the terror unleashed in the name of Islamic fundamentalism. India has been withstanding onslaughts of one kind or another for over a thousand years. Today the problem resulting from the *talibanisation* of Afghanistan and state sponsored terrorism on a worldwide scale is as much a global concern as it is for India and the neighbouring countries. At present it is still possible for the world to sanitise the locus of the emerging global menace. It is well known that more volunteers from other countries are being invited for *jehad* on a global scale. Once the contagion spreads, suicide bombers with explosives or even WMD would become commonplace in the cities of Europe and America, perhaps even China. Indians have been genetically inured to suffering. Their threshold of tolerance remains high. Not so the citizens of the developed world.

There has been talk, there is always such talk, of Person X or General Y being the bastion against fundamentalism and hence the need to make concessions or support that person. Otherwise the argument goes, the fundamentalists will have a field day. Arguments of this type, followed by concessions or compromises of the type suggested, actually prevent the emergence of leaders or interest groups who could mount an effective challenge or provide viable alternatives. At the very best it helps to postpone the inevitable. It has been the general experience that wherever hypotheses of this kind have led to policy changes, in accordance with the hypothesis advanced, the people of the nations concerned have seldom benefited. No real changes for the better have taken place.

In the case of Pakistan this type of thinking has taken center stage since quite some time. Benazir Bhutto sought the support of India (tacitly) and the West (openly) by claiming to be a bastion against military take-over. She ended up by strengthening the hands of the military. She too was opposed to fundamentalism. Yet her Interior Minister brought the Taliban into being. Now she can count on their support to take on the military should the need arise. The present military dictator makes the same plea. He is standing tall against fundamentalism, he says. In actual fact, all these stalwarts and many others beside them have allowed the radical groups to strengthen their hold by making compromises with them. They indulge in a holding action to keep their own party or self in power. They arrive at a *modus vivendi*. In reality, the radical groups need such bulwarks to flourish. They provide them a form of legitimacy and sustenance; because the bulwarks against fundamentalism have never any intention of meeting the challenge head on, to try and extirpate the evil from the soil. They give ground. They provide the fundamentalists the space in which to grow, by preventing other entities that could mount a more meaningful challenge from coming up.

Civilised norms cannot prevail in an uncivilised society. Nobody today would be willing to call the state of Pakistan a civilized society any more. In Pakistan (the proponents of terror and their supporters) the term includes all those who provide them space to grow, talk of the strengthening of religion. It is irreligion that is flourishing. The luminaries of religion in Pakistan and its environs are as removed from spirituality as is possible to be. Terror in the name of religion is being unleashed on the weak and the unprotected. It is being sanctified by the state by its incapacity or unwillingness to disarm, disband and outlaw these groups. The majority despises or fears them. They are sustained by military dictatorships and political dispensations that seek their support, in the process providing them the legitimacy they need to debouch from their ghettos. The demons of radicalism cannot be destroyed through accommodation. Well-wishers of Pakistan will have to go about organizing civil society and a new brand of leaders who are committed to eradicating the scourge from their soil. They will be required to be trained and armed to defend themselves and go after the radical elements and flush them out. There is no other way to save Pakistan from itself.

Afghanistan is in turmoil. Pakistan is in trouble. It is in deep trouble. India cannot remain unaffected. No nation on the subcontinent can remain unaffected. Kabul and the

Kabuliwalla remain as deeply etched in the collective psyche of the subcontinent as the *dohas* of Kabir. The destruction of Kabul, Kandahar and Herat diminishes the subcontinent. For centuries on end thunder in the form of invaders rolled down from the Hindukush into the plains of Punjab, all the way to Delhi. Hundreds of thousands of people who inhabited these lands were massacred. Untold suffering was visited upon them. After India and Pakistan became independent with the departure of the British no more invaders crossed the Khyber. Peace should finally have descended upon a people who had suffered so much in the centuries gone by. It didn't. The suffering now being visited upon the people of Afghanistan is deeper than any experienced in the past. Religion should have brought solace to the long-suffering people. Religion has become the basis for renewed killing. The widows and children of the slain weep. The killings continue. The worshippers of Allah do not know how to stop. Allah weeps.

2

Islam in a Cul de Sac

Science had its early beginnings in the Islamic civilisation between the 9th and 13th centuries, a time when Christian popes were burning 'witches' in the gloom of the Dark Ages. About seven hundred years ago, Islamic civilisation suffered a severe regression in its ability to acquire science and there have been no significant efforts at recovery since. Most Islamic traditionalists feel no regret and welcome the regression, believing that it helps preserve Islam from the corrupting and secular influences of Western civilisation where the validation of scientific truths depends on observation, experimentation and logic and not on any form of spiritual authority. Historically, Islamic civilisation has paid a heavy price for this failure, which has contributed to the retreat of Islamic civilisation and the ascendancy of the West[1].

Strong global currents, more powerful than the force of any individual nation or grouping, are shaping the world's future. Globalisation is merely one of the facets of this deep, upwelling movement that is reshaping the destiny of the world. Radical Islam or any form of fundamentalism represents a retrograde movement that will be swept away in the fullness of time. Meanwhile, the turbulence caused by these types of distortions in the human plane, in the societies where these take root, represents a cancerous growth, which can cause untold suffering to the societies where its spreads; unless it is extirpated before it reaches the terminal stage of malignancy.

It is amazing to see the setting up of the so-called ministries for the Prevention of Vice and the Promotion of Virtue coming up in the lands where fundamentalism has taken root. The irony of it all is obviously lost on the promoters of such institutions. The very fact that vice, as defined by them, has to be indefinitely suppressed through deprivation of individual liberties and visitation of unspeakable horrors, especially on the weaker sections, exposes the true face of these barbaric regimes.

Wherever these medieval systems operate it has been found that regardless of the passage of time they are almost never able to establish themselves in the hearts and minds of the people. By their very nature, they can never stabilise themselves except through perpetual terror and torture. The people of Pakistan must take note that the excesses of the Khomeini revolution in Iran at the beginning were almost as grave as the Taliban regime that had established itself over most of Afghanistan. What has been the outcome in Iran? The Iranian revolution - and the Iranian people's response to it a mere 20 years down the line - should be avidly studied in Pakistan. It has many lessons for the people of Pakistan, should they not wish to mortgage their future to a Taliban type dispensation in Pakistan.

Many from the Pakistan middle class fled the land of the pure, to go and settle in the lands of the impure. Not only have their dreams soured, the future as far as they can see, for themselves and their children, seems equally sterile. There is hardly anything to be proud of in their past since the time that Pakistan came into being. There is nothing to look forward to either. They have witnessed the creeping suffocation of most aspects of living that bring cheer to humdrum existence, like dancing, singing, healthy mixing of the sexes, general absence of taboos other than parental injunctions, celebrations of the festivals of spring and other joyous festivals celebrated unabashedly in an earlier era by their ancestors on the subcontinent. These simple activities that brought cheer to their lives are being gradually replaced by draconian, often barbaric, codes, almost each one of them a killjoy. So, the middle class build their future in distant lands while continuing to live in Pakistan in the hope that may be one day the dark period of the deadly combination of autocracy and theocracy will end. The way things are going this would appear to be a vain hope.

The horrors perpetrated by the Taliban on the hapless women of Afghanistan are by now too well known to require reiteration. What has not sunk in sufficiently into the people's consciousness is the fact that these atrocities are spilling over into other areas of the subcontinent amongst the Islamic populations. Just a handful of zealots are able to terrorise whole segments of population who may be viscerally opposed to such draconian injunctions at the behest of the votaries of violence; who have neither the authority nor the right to enforce such medieval norms. Recently, radical Islamist elements threw acid on girls in Srinagar for not sporting the veil. Earlier, a young girl was shot dead for non-compliance. Cases of this nature are on the rise in Pakistan, Bangladesh, the Kashmir Valley and elsewhere. Regardless of where these atrocities are perpetrated the fount for the spread of the demonic fervor are the radical Islamic camps in Pakistan and Afghanistan.

It is for the people of Pakistan to take note of what is being perpetrated in their name. Unless they themselves sit up and see the situation for what it is they too will suffer unspeakable horrors in the name of Islam. Before it is too late they have to take note of their situation and the direction in which their state is being pushed. They should pay heed to what John Ruskin said in this regard: 'You may either win your peace or buy it; win it, by resistance to evil; buy it, by compromise with evil'. The followers of Islam everywhere, and more so in Pakistan, must ask themselves the question as to whether the Prophet of Islam and their religion sanctions the throwing of acid on young girls or shooting them dead so that other girls can be terrorised into submission. Islam is not being threatened from without. It is being threatened from within. It is being pushed by radical elements into a form of sterility from which it will find it difficulty to re-emerge. Islam of the moderate and tolerant variety can certainly not be in danger. It is the spirit of Islam that is being attacked, not by supposed enemies, but by elements that are as far removed from godliness as is possible to be. The responsibility for the degradation of Islam by such methods lies squarely on the shoulders of every citizen of Pakistan. They are alive to what has been happening. An ostrich-like policy of burying their heads in the sand will help neither the cause of Islam nor that of Pakistan in the long run. Time is running out for them. It is still not too late to turn back.

The carnage in Kashmir brings out starkly the ravages that continue to afflict the subcontinent fifty years after the departure of the colonial masters. The pictures of defenseless women and children massacred in cold blood would not have failed to bestir all those who beheld the scenes of the grisly massacre. The acts were dastardly, tragic and senseless. It will not help the cause of those who perpetrated the outrage. All in the name of Allah, Allah weeps. Fifty years of senseless fighting has not yet convinced the establishment in Pakistan that nothing can be gained through war with India. Neither Pakistan nor Islam is gaining any advantage from it. To the contrary, should this trend continue it could end up destroying Pakistan. Allah could never have sanctioned such monstrosities. The very first chapter of the Qur'an has the second verse as *Al-Rehman al-Rahim* (The Compassionate, the Merciful). The first verse too carries the sense of compassion when it describes Allah as *Rabb al-'Alamin* (i.e. Sustainer of the whole world). The concept of sustenance of the whole world itself is based on His Mercy and Compassion for everything He has created. In fact *rahmah* is so central to Allah's existence that it embraces all that exists in the universe (*wasi`at kulla shayin*) [2].

In fact He sent His Messenger Muhammad also as the Mercy of the World. Thus the Prophet of Islam also represents universal mercy. As the Messenger of Allah he is representative of His Mercy and hence the Prophet himself is known as *rahmatan lil 'alamin* (Mercy of the worlds). Anyone who is cruel and insensitive towards the sufferings of others cannot be the Prophet's true follower in any sense. It is a great pity that other than the Sufis and their followers many Muslims have forgotten the emphasis of the Holy Qur'an on the quality of compassion. The Sufis lay tremendous stress on compassion. Their very fundamental doctrine is what is called *sulh-i-kul* i.e. peace with all, which means no violence and no aggressiveness. The majority of Muslims of course follow the Sufi approach. It is only fringe groups who keep harping on *jehad*. There is no verse in the Qur'an that permits violence for conquering territory or for achieving power. In fact war has been qualified in the Qur'an by the words *fi' sabilillah* i.e. in the way of Allah.

The agony of Afghanistan, which in a way is linked to the present tragedy, is also the tragedy of the subcontinent. The latest discoveries of the extent of the Harappan sites indicate that unity existed from time immemorial. Many of the kings of Delhi before the advent of the British came from the region that is now Afghanistan and Central Asia. During the three centuries of the Moghul rule, interaction with the Afghan people was at its height. Coming to the present times, there would not be many amongst the older generation who were not familiar with the lore of the *Kabuliwala*.

It requires a special type of opaqueness not to be able to discern the international trends in the age of globalisation. The subcontinent is sandwiched invitingly between the giant economies to its East and West. It is the next prize to be picked. If the countries of South Asia continue on their present course they will have united only in the folly of ensuring that the peoples of the subcontinent become subjected to a bondage worse than any suffered by the peoples during the colonial domination earlier.

While parallels continue to be drawn between the most recent military take-over and the earlier ones, the people of Pakistan who have some awareness about the regional and global reality, must realise that drawing comparisons between the earlier and the present military regime is fraught with dangerous consequences. In the case of the earlier military dictatorships in Pakistan during the Cold War much of the Western world as well as the Muslim countries - often taking their cue from the former - looked at Pakistan as an ally against Soviet expansionism. They were not unduly perturbed that democracy had been put on the back burner, as long as Pakistan's policies were directed towards supporting the interests of the non-communist powers. This is no longer the case. The Western powers are now looking at Pakistan with considerable misgiving, while strengthening selected segments of their military for their own ends. Many, if not most, of the Muslim countries look at Pakistan with apprehension, occasionally with hostility.

A fundamental question that the citizens of professedly Islamic states should be asking themselves is whether modernity is compatible with orthodoxy. An analysis of the subject would show that it clearly is not. It is not limited to orthodoxy in Islam. It applies to all orthodoxies. Nature continues to evolve. Life is evolving. The universe is evolving. Evolution is essential for any vibrant, living system. Either it evolves or it perishes. The human body evolves. The mind evolves. Through the centuries governance systems have evolved. Hence to maintain that a clutch of clergyman should be given the power to hold back progress is a proposition that is fundamentally abhorrent to any evolving system. In days gone by - and even in the modern era - evolved beings in almost all societies were generally those individuals who through their spirituality and conduct in life had won the respect, admiration, adulation and love of their fellow human beings. A common feature of all such evolved beings, through the ages, has been their respect for life and all life forms, their self-denial, their wisdom and compassion. Of all these attributes compassion has invariably stood out as the dominant attribute.

When one examines the attributes of the present clergymen who have helped to create much of the unrest that now engulfs many of the Muslim societies – and other societies where such people have come to the fore – it will be found that they have been mostly lacking in the attributes of evolved human beings of the earlier days. They are singularly lacking in compassion. Their words do not soothe. They arouse. Their actions and sermons release negative, destructive energies in the people that they have gathered around them. Except for the observance of rituals there is hardly anything in their personal life worth emulating. They are political animals in religious garb that have helped to contaminate their environment. The question that intelligent people in Muslim societies should ask themselves, and each other is, as to how such people have been allowed to accumulate power – limited entirely to the temporal domain – that is propelling their societies towards imminent self-destruction. Is it by default, indifference or apathy - to organize themselves and take their own destinies as individuals and that of their societies in directions that do not lead to self-destruction, but allow for a more harmonious existence with societies with whom they are obliged to co-dwell in the 21st century.

When one talks of religious leaders and spiritually enlightened people the figures that come to mind are Mahatma Gandhi, Martin Luther King, Mother Theresa, Dalai Lama and the like. Each one of them worked to uplift their people. Each one of them was first and foremost a humanist. All of them exuded compassion and kindness. Each one of them shunned violence. Such is the nature of religious figures. Do the people in Pakistan, who are responding to the call of *jehad*, seriously hold the view that any of the clergymen who have given the call are in the same mould? Are they not, in effect, rabble-rousers? Do they not spit venom from the pulpit? Therefore, the parents who are bequeathing their children into the hands of such devilish beings, crazed by their lust for political power, are they not condemning their children to a life of repressed development. The products coming out of these seminaries are full of hatred for their fellow human beings beyond the pale of Islam, as defined by the Mullahs who run these seminaries. There can hardly be any gains for the students who come out of these institutions and for the state that supports these institutions. There can only be pain, both for the programmed misanthropes and the state itself. Either way: pain inflicted upon others or pain suffered due to the response in kind.

While insisting on an Islamic state in Pakistan - lately at its intolerant worst - Pakistan has moved away from the vision of Jinnah, the founder of Pakistan. It would be recalled that Jinnah wanted Pakistan to be a secular state with a Muslim majority, but where all religions would be given full freedom and treated as equals in the new state. Towards this end he had tried to entice Junagarh and Jodhpur states to opt for Pakistan. In insisting on the ideological hypothesis that the basis of its nationhood could only be religion – the Muslim religion – Pakistan chose to go on a path that would definitely put it in confrontation with India; from which the state of Pakistan was torn asunder when the colonial power relinquished its hold over India. The ideological principle that only religion could be the basis of nationhood has created a major dilemma for rapprochement on the subcontinent. The ethnic and linguistic difficulties in Pakistan result largely from these absurd claims that if you are a Muslim you cannot be a Baluchi or Sindhi and so on.

It has to be remembered that *madrasa* education, in itself, helped to fill an important gap on the subcontinent for centuries. The products of the *madrasas* were generally God-fearing, law abiding and decent citizens. The distortion of *madrasa* education for irreligious purposes, for engendering hatred and violence in young minds to the exclusion of modernising and humanising education, is a comparatively recent phenomenon, the locus for which again happens to be Pakistan. From Pakistan it has spread to many parts of the subcontinent, Afghanistan, Central Asia and elsewhere, with generous Saudi backing and lately drug monies. Mention must be made of the fact that even the Saudi government is now not very comfortable with the extremism and violence that has become the hallmark of the products of the *madrasas* being churned out. It is indeed a far cry from the *madrasas* of the medieval ages during Muslim rule when these *madrasas* were centres of higher knowledge. The decline in the concept and quality of *madrasa* education commenced under British rule in as much as the scientific content of the teaching imparted declined and state patronage, which was available in earlier times, was discontinued. The poor Muslims had no option but to fall back on *madrasa* education. It neither augurs well for Muslims nor for nations of the subcontinent that the *madrasas* are looked upon as centres of fundamentalism - sponsored by ISI funds to carry out its divisive and anti-social activities. This trend, should it continue unchecked, will debase the very concept of *madrasa* education for generations to come. Pakistan society when compared to its counterparts in India is becoming intellectually sterile. There is superficial gloss. Real talent or genius cannot flourish in sterile soil.

All over the world, in most societies, there has been tremendous effort towards women's emancipation and women's empowerment. Women are going out and holding their own. They are contributing to society. Not so in fundamentalist type dispensations. The brutalisers of women, who push them back towards the Middle Ages, talk about the evil ways of advanced societies, the so-called decadent societies. Whatever be the case, every person has a right to choose his or her future. It cannot be an imposition of a few usurpers of religious orthodoxy who decide what is good for others. In most cases they are oblivious of global currents, of scientific debates, of the many cross currents that describe and define today's world. Keeping the other gender in perpetual physical and mental slavery is not a religious mandate sanctioned by any religion. It is a negation of human values and the freedom of thought. The very fact that all such dispensations have to keep their hold through perpetual terror exposes the true nature of the dispensation. Socio-economic advancement is taking place through women's emancipation in various segments of South Asian society. Away from obscurantist influences, progress is more rapid in India. Elsewhere it can be seen that where religion is being pressed, or press-ganged into service, ostentatious religiosity is on the increase, spirituality on the decline. Segments of society referred to, as fundamentalists are essentially those people who feel threatened by social movements and changes sweeping the world. Since the force of modern, scientific education would always remain stronger for the younger generation, were they to be given a choice, the orthodox elements find it expedient to denounce it as being contrary to the religious tenets that they uphold. It is axiomatic that brute radicalism ends up by producing the law of the jungle, which then supplants the spirit, if not the letter, of Islamic law. Thanks to the support of the ruling elite and the military establishment from time to time, the Muslim clergy realise that for perhaps the first time in history they are close to grasping political power. It being so near at hand, it beckons maddeningly and distorts their vision.

In recent years there has been a lot of talk of the Muslim *ummah*. Many others referred to it as pan-Islamic revival or the Muslim brotherhood. What does all this mean to the common man? How does being part of the so-called global Muslim brotherhood help to improve his living conditions in the backward, poverty- stricken regions of Bihar and UP in India or similar regions in Pakistan and Bangladesh; likewise, how is his lot improved in Indonesia? The Saudis have spent billions of dollars since oil prices were raised, pumping money into Western industries and real estate in the West. Tens of billions of dollars more have been spent in procuring sophisticated armaments and keeping the military industry complex in the West afloat. Sizeable amounts were spent in fomenting *jehad* in Pakistan and in helping the Taliban throughout the 1990s. Does any Muslim in the subcontinent expect to share the oil wealth of the Arabs through investments in infrastructure development in the backward regions of Pakistan, India or Bangladesh? Has any person of the so-called pan-Islamic brotherhood ever paused to think as to against whom the sophisticated arms procured by Saudi Arabia or, for that matter, the other Gulf countries would be used: against the Chinese; against Russia; against America and the Western Alliance?

They will be used, as they have been used throughout history: in decimating their neighbours in the region; for protecting their wealth; or for extending their influence beyond their countries' borders. Human nature does not change. It certainly does not change overnight. Nations do not change either. They pursue their own interest as deemed fit by the ruling elite of the period, mainly to retain hold on power and to pursue their own agenda. What is true of South Asia, the Middle East or Central Asia is true for the rest of the world. Only naïve, deprived segments of the population, lacking in modern education and health facilities, can be influenced into such thinking by their ruling establishments or the Muslim clergy, to retain their hold on the people with the promise of a rosier dawn. Only people who have suffered historical discontinuities can fall a prey to this type of thinking after they have been sufficiently dissociated from their past heritage.

It is possible for a Muslim to find kinship, linguistic and cultural affinities, common food habits and other similarities with people in the region. The same Muslim, if transplanted to Arabia or Xinjiang in China amongst fellow Muslims, would be like a fish out of water. He will find that the Arab or Chinese Muslims are very different from the Indian and Pakistani Muslims. Few Pakistanis have even paused to think whether any Arab will marry his daughter to a Pakistani or Indian Muslim. Almost never. The Muslim from the subcontinent can be a servant. Hardly ever a relative. Muslim women of the subcontinent are taken as maids and kept women, or chattel for the wealthy Arabs. The Muslim clergy and ruling elite have been co-opted into the scheme of things by large financial doles so that they learn to keep their mouths shut and continue to talk of pan-Islamism and Muslim brotherhood. It is a travesty of religion. It is a travesty of fact. It is an insult to the penury of the people, who might have retained a shred of dignity.

There is a more fundamental question that requires to be answered when talking of Muslim brotherhood. How is it different from the brotherhood of Man? As science and technology change the very nature of our societies and the world faces planetary stresses of a type that can end up by destroying the world, what should intelligent human beings extol? How do they distinguish from one brotherhood to another? If there is a Muslim brotherhood, why should not there be similar exclusionary brotherhoods for other people? Should these other brotherhoods take up the same chant, 'kill or destroy people who are not a part of our own brotherhood'? One can go further. Should a brotherhood of the Masonic Lodge supersede the brotherhood of religion? Should the brotherhood of narco-traffickers, drug-peddlers and racketeers indulging in the flesh trade be a more elevated brotherhood than the religious type? (Apparently, it is the case). Does the brotherhood of caste take precedence over the brotherhood of religion or whatever other exclusive grouping? What about language ethnicity? Where should it come in the pecking order of the cauldron of hatreds - and exclusivities - taking shape in many parts of the world?

The perversities of religious dogma in the 21st century are being mobilised to whip up emotions as a means to amass influence, wealth or political power. People who preach such hatred and exclusivity are as far removed from human decency and compassion as is possible to be.

They are busy fanning the flames of hatred and stoking the fires of genocide and fratricide. They are distorting the vision of young people who come into their clutches and degrading their humanity. They are defiling the earth and pushing their religion into a *cul de sac*. Tragically for the world they do not belong to any one community or religion.

The current US led offensive against global terrorism, directed mainly at terrorism sponsored by radical Islamists on the one hand and the reaction to the American action in the form of growing anti-Americanism in the Muslim world on the other, are a prelude to violent civilisation clashes, whether people like to admit it or not. Whatever the disclaimers, and howsoever unintended, or intentional, the effects, the fact remains that the Muslims all over the world are generally targeting the West; and the American led Christian West feels obliged to eradicate the radical Islamists at source. The very thought of a repeat of September 11 events taking place ever again in any Western country would give their establishments nightmares, for a long time to come. On the face of it the bloodletting that is likely to follow appears to be inevitable. The voice of moderation is likely to be ignored by hotheads on both sides.

The lead elements pushing confrontation in the Western world as well as the Muslim world are not people who have an open mind. For each side it is a war being fought against evil; the evil being personified by key personae of the opponents. Whatever the outcome and whatever the duration of the struggle the fact remains that it represents a vast churning. To put it in another way, a defining moment in the histories of the two civilisations that appear to be clashing. Actually the word civilisation is a misnomer. In the present case the clash is occurring due to the uncivilised nature of the respective movements pushing their societies towards a clash. At a more basic level it is a clash for political and economic dominance: on the one hand for global dominance; on the other for getting hold of the levers of power - in Muslim countries - by the orthodox theologians. Surprisingly, should the latter gain control the clash will end. Rather it will be postponed to another time. Meanwhile, accommodations will be reached so that the radical clergy are allowed a free hand within their societies to turn the clock back a few centuries. Hence, the clash that is taking place is both within the societies, i.e., the liberal urge versus diehard orthodoxy; and without, i.e., with countries or systems – embedded mainly in the West, who are likely to challenge the internal hegemony of the orthodoxy clergy.

Whatever the nature and duration of the struggle a positive outcome that could be in the offing is that the average person in the societies under stress, both in the West and in the East, is being forced to come to grips with global realities and perceptions long ignored. People are being obliged to reevaluate their positions in society, the impositions that they face in their respective societies, as also the future outlook if un-accommodative and illiberal postures continue to be adopted by any segment in the shrinking global village. This individual exploration, though tentative and swamped by the radical militancy to begin with, represents deep societal churning from which a new and more rational order is bound to emerge; for reestablishing the social cohesion of societies which had suffered a breakdown in the second half of the 20th century.

In as far as it relates to Islamic societies the deep churning must bring to the fore the question of gender equality. Are these societies going to emerge with a humanising, gender friendly outlook or are they going to regress into their suppressive gender inequalities as witnessed in the regions where orthodoxy holds sway? Gender inequality has nothing to do with Islam or the Quran. It is slavery perpetrated by the males on their female counterparts resulting in one half of the population not being able to participate in the life of the community, the country or the emerging global society. It is male chauvinism at its worst.

For a long time Muslim societies, through repression and the shutting out of modern education, science and technology, have managed to get away with double standards. In their own countries they insist upon imposing their so-called superior puritanical and moral standards upon outsiders. In their turn they have no qualms in going to other countries and demanding every freedom available in democratic societies, even to the extent of undermining these societies. It allows them the liberty to practice their trade or live their lives in any manner that pleases them, including to turn into suicide bombers against societies that nurtured them. A mullah sitting in Delhi can boldly support terrorist actions and still live freely, without let or hindrance. He can organise processions, indulge in inflammatory, treasonous oratory and yet expect to utilise the liberal traditions of the society in which he lives to remain free.

The present crisis provides an unexpected opportunity to reexamine conditions in which obscurantist elements freely indulge in suppressing the weaker sex and denying gender equality, a violation of universal human rights - all in the name of a spurious religious morality. Since the imposition is maintained through coercion and open violence, under antiquated laws that would not be acceptable under any rational or humanistic dispensation, these need to be reevaluated.

To perpetuate their hold the orthodox clergy insist on establishing a state based on religious ideology and then prevent any new legislation that could moderate some of the anachronisms that had crept in from ages past, even from the pre-medieval period, from being enacted. Open discussion is not permitted. Anyone who questions the anachronistic interpretations commits a serious crime. Change is frowned upon by a handful of self-appointed repositories of wisdom; who do not realise that such arrogance is itself the greatest sin. They expect a religious state to not only implement these laws rigorously but also punish severely all those who advocate change. They have been brought up on dogmas. By closing their minds to nourishing inputs provided by other sources, that could enrich the giver and the receiver through cross-fertilisation, they often fall into grave error, by defending the indefensible. It would be recalled that both Christianity - and the European society that adopted Christianity - was greatly influenced by Greek thinkers. Their cherished dogmas that continued well into the second millennium, like the earth being flat and at the centre of the universe and the sun going round it, were acquired from Greek thinkers and philosophers. At some point these became integral part of Christian and Islamic doctrines. Challenges to the dogmas upheld by the church and clergy could be punished with death. When Galileo challenged this dogma he was punished and made to recant. It took the Renaissance to free the church and the people from the mental straitjacket of those earlier beliefs that could not be held for long once inquiring and open minds were able to savour the refreshing inputs made available through scientific advances. By accepting the changes, albeit belatedly, the Church was not diminished. It adopted the changes and proceeded to revitalise itself and the society that it nurtured. What happened in Europe during that period was not peculiar to the Christian church. A broad spectrum analysis will show that new scientific discoveries, social and political changes, no matter how beneficial to the people were fiercely opposed by established religious authorities in the name of religion; and the votaries of change persecuted till the time that the fullness of the new idea could no longer be turned away by narrow dogmas of the earlier period. Islam is today once again at a watershed. The direction that Muslim societies wish to take should be decided upon openly after due deliberations by *all* segments of the emerging societies. A handful of people cannot be the arbiters of resistance to change simply because they are able to tyrannise their populations into silence and submission. No religion, society or culture can call itself civilised without embodying compassion, arguably the most spiritual of all qualities. Any religion, society or culture that allows hatred and intolerance to come to the fore is doomed – not only in the physical sense, but also in the metaphysical sense that distinguishes between being and nothingness. When hatred becomes the *leitmotif* of any society, sterility enters the soul of that society. It would then be well on the way to self-destruction.

Throughout the ages civilised societies in most parts of the world have functioned such that different segments of the society attended to their respective pursuits in a manner that they did not necessarily intrude upon one another to the detriment of any segment. A society that is harmoniously blended leads to a better whole, whether in the form of a kingdom, a community or a state. In the case of Pakistan a distortion appeared with the advent of Zia-ul-Haq. Theology that was generally confined to the seminaries made its appearance in greater number of educational institutions and on to the street; till a state was reached where it attempted to overwhelm the other organisations of the state in a manner that would be regarded as regressive for any modern society. This process carried to excess can damn the future of Pakistan substantively and comprehensively.

There is a tendency to overdo the scholastic interpretation of the Quran in the 21st century. The average person has fallen into the theological trap while discussing radicalism especially of the Islamic variety. This applies to governments and intellectuals. Most people have a fair idea of what is wrong and what is right. Killing of innocent people, women and children is an abominable act. These acts are morally repugnant to any humanistic creed. One does not have to quote the scriptures to condemn them. Such condemnation automatically flows from the viewpoint of commonsense, jurisprudence or from any rational plane. No civilised society can sponsor or tolerate such behaviour and still call itself civilised. Therefore, there should not be any need to go into theology to bring out their moral indefensibility. By the same token, it is amazing that suicide missions resulting in the deaths of innocent people have been made out to be passports to heaven. Elementary commonsense tells one that suicide is a sinful act; and where such a foolhardy act results in the death of innocent people it is a sure passport to purgatory, whichever way one looks at it. The youth who undertake these missions can never be considered martyrs to any cause. They are naïve and gullible youngsters imbued with hatred from an early age to further the geopolitical ambitions of people dreaming of political or religious dominance on a global scale. It is incomprehensible that any text of any great religion of the world allows for such interpretation.

It is inconceivable that educated, learned and wise people actually allow the belief to be propagated that committing atrocities on innocent people by blowing up oneself in the midst of a crowd will lead the person committing the heinous act to heaven and straight into the laps of beautiful `houris'. It is such an unpardonable offense on the part of the programmers who propagate this view as to defy mere condemnation. On many occasions, the people who passed such orders were (themselves) found to be mercenaries and released criminals who had gone up the militancy ladder through their tactical skills and unflinching cruelty. If any group of wise people, scholars, or respected religious leaders were to examine them it would be found that one of the common features of such programmers was their near complete absence of humour or humaneness. It never struck enlightened Muslim opinion anywhere in the world to challenge the moral authority of these people to lull the youth of Islam into such beliefs. Acts of this nature could never be sanctioned by a great religion like Islam or, for that matter, any other religion. It is a travesty of faith. It is a blight on the practitioners of a great religion that distortions of this type are allowed to sully their sacred faith at the hands of mullahs and mercenaries. Going just a little further into the mentality of the teachers and handlers of the young people being motivated into hatred - followed by self-destructive acts - it will be found that it is invariably the young people who are being deprived of their youth to further the ambitions of their masters.

The cynical exploitation of young boys becomes clearer when it is realised that older people who would no longer be able to attract young women benefit by sending eligible young men to their death. It helps if there is less competition when they themselves dip into the pool of young women available for replenishing their stocks.

The discussion on Islam brings out the fact that the radicalisation of a great religion is taking place on account of the inability of the vast majority of the people living in these countries to counter the machinations of people seeking political dominance through the spread of religious orthodoxy. The excerpt that follows sums up the situation admirably:

"Yet, for all the cruelty and obscurantism associated with religion, hidden within the great traditions of faith are precious resources for the future welfare of humanity and these are too important to be abandoned to the extremists".[3]

That is exactly what is taking place. The fringe elements 'act'. The silent majority just sits and 'talks'. Intellectuals debate the issues at conferences and make condemnatory noises. The extremists take no notice of them. They continue to 'act'. The tragedy of Kashmir is in essence the tragedy of Islam in the 21st century. The fight in Kashmir is ostensibly a fight between Pakistan and India. In reality the fight in Kashmir is between a humanistic creed and obscurantist beliefs that should have disappeared with the Dark Ages. The dehumanising injunctions issued from time to time by a retrogressive orthodoxy on a population cowering under terror is reminiscent of the *auto da fe* of the worst period of the Inquisition. By attempting to destroy Sufism in Kashmir the radical Islamists are pushing Islam into a *cul de sac.*

This leads to some very pertinent questions on the interface between Islam and Kashmir.

The first of these propositions questions:

"Has the *talibanisation* of Afghanistan brought peace and prosperity to the region"?

The next question, following from the first:

"Has the creeping *talibanisation* of Pakistan and its army brought peace and prosperity to the region'?

It follows that the next question to be posed inquires:

"Will the hypothetical *talibanisation* of Kashmir bring peace and prosperity to Kashmir"?

Therefore, the subsequent question leaps up:

"Should India seriously countenance with equanimity the *talibanisation* of the Vale of Kashmir"?

What is being witnessed today could conceivably be the second and final regression of Islam in case the liberal Islamic elements are unable to face the challenge mounted by radical Islam. There are over four hundred million adherents of the Islamic faith on the subcontinent. They have to take up the challenge posed to the magnificence of their religion by the radical fringes of Islam. Instead of getting involved in obscure texts and the interpretations that vary from age to age they too must pose themselves some simple, soul-searching questions:

"Does Allah, the Merciful, the Just, require terror – of the type being unleashed on innocent women and children in the name of religion – to add to His glory"?

"Is the programmed violence being unleashed by the petty myrmidons of tyranny – through the *deeni madaris* – embellishing, in any way, the magnificence of the teachings of the Quran"?

"If the answer to the first two questions is not in the affirmative then *why* are the *silent majority* of Muslims on the subcontinent *silent*. Why are they allowing their religion to be so denigrated by people who are using it as a tool to capture political power"?

There would be many in Pakistan, especially in the *jehadi* fold who would be holding the belief that the World Trade Centre (WTC) attacks were just punishment for American haughtiness. There is no doubt that the economic costs of the bombings to the US have been high. It has had a very major impact on the insurance and airlines sectors besides the economic costs of reconstruction. The talented people who were killed in the Twin Towers represented the *crème de la crème* of the companies who had their offices in the WTC. While *Al Qaeda* may congratulate itself for having inflicted such loss on the mighty USA they never paused to take into account before going ahead with their ill-conceived act the consequences that would be visited upon their brethren in and around Afghanistan due to the inevitable US retaliation. It would be naïve for their leaders to suppose that such retaliation would strengthen their cause. Although Islamic *jehad* of the variety preached by them has an emotive appeal for many young people in the Islamic world, especially amongst the poorer sections of society, it does not follow therefrom that once the global response patterns permeate down to the rank and file they will continue to motivate them to the same extent as before. There is an even bigger issue involved, which exposes the narrow-mindedness and self-centredness of the indoctrinated followers of Islamic *jehad*. They would have been aware that USA is the leading economic power of the world. Linked to their allies in the developed countries they control an enormous amount of the global wealth. When the American economy suffers it has, to varying degrees, a far more deleterious ripple effect on the economies of developing nations. It means that the elements who committed the September 11 outrage - and their sponsors - cynically disregarded the effect of the economic hardships that would be suffered by possibly hundreds of million of their brethren, both Islamic and non-Islamic, in the countries already suffering from want and deprivation. The US economy is larger perhaps than the combined economies of the Third World. Being a rich country its ability to absorb the impact of an economic downturn is far greater than that of the poor countries. Fledgling exports and tourism and travel will be affected in a big way. Countries around the world will be obliged to spend far more for security at airports, railway stations, bus terminals and other places where people congregate in large numbers. These are all unproductive costs for the developing countries who are unable to afford further diminution in their near starvation wages. Insurance companies will charge higher premiums. All these are effects that will be visited upon peoples of the Third World, which are the milieu that radical Islamists come from. They have dealt a bigger flow to their own kind than the one inflicted on the USA. The people of Pakistan who were the prime movers towards the spread of radical Islam must sit back and think things through for themselves. They can ill afford to leave their future well being in the hands of the military and the mullahs. More of the same simply will not do any more.

It defies comprehension that millions upon millions of Muslims who have been witnessing the indoctrination of people in their tender years have not mustered the courage or the cohesion to act decisively in the face of an activity that is the very antithesis of Islam. There is an unpardonable waste of young lives being used as canon fodder to further the ambitions of the firebrands who have been proliferating in Pakistan and, thereafter, in Afghanistan. If the US is in occupation of certain military bases, which have been given to them by the governments of the concerned countries, irrespective of whether they are popular governments or otherwise, the answer certainly does not lie in terrorist acts that send the younger generation to certain death. The US is a superpower. Its behaviour is no different from that of the mighty powers of earlier centuries. It conforms to type. At the dawn of the new century it has assumed the shape of a colossus. It has begun to exhibit the 'nature' of a colossus. What exactly is the nature of a colossus? The nature of a colossus is that it begins to develop an appetite for aggrandisement. By making this statement it is not the intention here to attribute any malign intent to USA's leadership. The discussion is on historical phenomenon. They closely resemble natural phenomenon. Throughout history its colossi have, almost without exception, manifested this urge. Kingdoms that became large grew into empires. Empires, after consolidation, started becoming larger and larger through a process of conquest till they assumed gigantic proportions i.e. they had become fit to burst. The 19th and 20th centuries were no exception. The British Empire grew so large that ultimately it had to give way. The Soviet Empire is a more recent case. The lone superpower, unless it shows self-restraint, will come to the bursting point any time in the first half of this century. This time around, the difference would be that when the explosion occurs it could possibly destroy much of the world as well. It is the reality of nuclear weapons and weapons of mass destruction. The great powers of the 18th and 19th centuries, essentially the European powers England and France, were in occupation – physical occupation as opposed to stationing of troops at the behest of the concerned governments – of the Arabian Peninsula and the Middle East. One does not recall similar acts of terror in the name of *jehad* to oust them.

Politics and religion should not be allowed to mix in the modern world. It neither benefits religion nor the politics of a state. It is one thing to encourage people to be God-fearing and religious in their daily lives. It is quite another to mobilise people to interfere in governance activities that are as far removed from theological precepts of earlier millennia as is possible to be. When the two get mixed they create turbulence in all spheres that they touch. It is for the intelligentsia of Pakistan to now question the very basis of the belief inculcated in the minds of the very young that suicide missions against innocent civilians could lead to heaven. Should they allow the perpetuation of the myth of virgins awaiting the perpetrators of such acts they abet in making a mockery of their religion. Such shibboleths cannot withstand any rational, scholastic or intelligent religious scrutiny in this day and age.

The Islamic radical groups have been single mindedly targeting America, blaming it for many of the ills afflicting the Islamic world. The proximate causes for the Al Qaeda attacks mentioned, *inter alia*, the positioning of US troops in the Arabian Peninsula and US support for Israel. Other grievances have also been thrown in from time to time. None of these can be discounted while examining the growth of terrorist groups in the Islamic world. For many people there may be a belief in the justification of some of these charges leveled against the USA. A deeper analysis, while not discounting these grievances, would go on to show that many of the ills afflicting the Muslim world cannot be laid entirely at the door of the US. In most of the Muslim countries modern education that could raise the standards of these societies has been deliberately put on the back burner. The winds of change have not been allowed in, not because they would corrupt the people exposed to them but because it would free the people from the obscurantist beliefs and mores being imposed on them through religious terror. They are being prevented from making comparisons and deciding for themselves. Such restrictions challenge the mental capacity of a whole generation to think for itself, when one questions their ability to choose their own way forward. The Muslim nations will continue to remain backward, in spite of America, till perhaps well into the century till their existence becomes a matter of indifference for the rest of the world on account of their backwardness as is the case today with some of the tribes deep in the Amazon. The main reason for this backwardness would be the relegation of their women, i.e., half their population into a state of perpetual inferiority and unproductiveness in the modern sense of the word.

Neither USA, nor the West, nor any other country can be blamed for the income disparities within the Muslim world. The Organisation of Islamic Conference (OIC) meets have generally been used to denounce the enemies of Islam. They have seldom been used to debate issues related to removing poverty in the most backward regions of the Muslim world. The oil revenues have been utilized in the most wasteful manner imaginable – in subsidizing backward educational institutions that actually condemn the youth to permanent incompatibility with the market or the modern world. It has been used for profligacy; the case of the scion of a royal family of Brunei is a case in point. The billions and billions of dollars wasted upon frivolities, yachts and orgies have seldom been condemned by the OIC or the bin Ladens of the Muslim world. It is possible to go on in this vein. The fact remains that it is far easier to blame others for one's own failings, much more difficult to look within. The USA could conceivably be blamed for some of the ills being visited upon the Muslim world. It does not warrant, by any stretch of imagination, the launching of terror attacks or *jehad* on that country or any other country in the manner of the WTC bombings of September 11, 2001.

3

Deconstruction of the Pakistan State

Deconstruction of the state as it exists in Pakistan becomes an ineluctable necessity on account of the existential dilemma that its continuance in the present form poses for the people of Pakistan and the global community. Major structural flaws have developed. The dismantling process has to be a controlled one to the extent possible to prevent cataclysmic upheavals that could last decades and result in the break up of Pakistan. In stable countries, especially democracies, the army provides the depth for state security. In Pakistan, the army itself is fast becoming the state. As opposed to earlier dictatorships this time round the army is becoming all pervasive. The civil structure of the country is being deliberately dismantled. Even the judiciary has expressed concern over the army encroaching upon its functions. In earlier times, when the army was obliged to pull back due to public pressure after prolonged army misrule, a fall back was available in the form of the civilian bureaucracy. Political parties waiting in the wings were able to mobilise their supporters to occupy the governing niche. Presently, the alternative to army rule is radical Islam, a prospect looked at with dismay by the people of Pakistan and the world. The global community and various groupings in Pakistan will have to join hands to release Pakistan from the clutches of creeping *talibanisation*. Pakistan has two choices – either to go in for controlled reconstruction or await a civil war and subsequent break up. Meanwhile, should the menace of radical Islam break existing bounds the global community will have no choice but to annihilate it *in situ*, by whatever means at its disposal.

What Pakistan has today is what the civil and military bureaucracy had been trying to establish since the nineteen fifties and which Iskander Mirza, sometime President of the country, had first articulated as 'controlled democracy' as being the need of Pakistan. In one form or another it has remained the operative mandate for the Pakistan army whether in or out of the direct exercise of power. Therefore, all governance has to be within the limits set by the establishment. Although not stated in so many words, the framework includes the proviso that greater centralisation – concentration of power in Islamabad – must continue to prevail. The idea was put into practice in the time of Field Marshal Ayub Khan and met an ignominious fate after his departure. The people began to perceive that Ayub's idea that devolution of power must go down to the districts through his concept of 'basic democracies' would lead to the provinces of Pakistan being bypassed. The Centre wanted to deal directly with the districts. The idea being revived now in a slightly altered form has been floated before and has always been met with suspicion by the provinces. An earlier experiment led to the dire consequences of 1971 and the break up of the country. It would be short sighted in the extreme to repeat the experiment. Unless the political system ensures a genuine federal structure and the provinces given genuine autonomy, further break up of the country could ensue.

That there is and has been a fundamental antagonism between Hindus and Muslims in the subcontinent since the advent of Islam is a fact. It is a legacy of history over which the present generation did not have control. In India there is a determined effort by the majority of the people of the two largest religions to bridge the religious divide and live in harmony for building a prosperous India that, by extension, transfers into a stable, prosperous and harmonious subcontinent, from Colombo to Kabul. Fundamentalism has raised its ugly head in India as well. Fortunately for India its people have rejected the brand of Hindu fundamentalism that came to the fore in the closing decades of the 20th century. The Indian electorate has expressed its displeasure in no uncertain terms. Indian democracy acts as a corrective.

No such corrective obtains in Pakistan. By making religion the basis of its dispute with India the military-mullah combine in Pakistan is pushing the country on a collision course not only with India, but with much of the world that has no time for the type of obscurantism being practised and propagated from Pakistan and Afghanistan. The bulk of the military leaders of Pakistan, devoid of liberal education or outlook, are unable to grasp the fundamentals of the major problems confronting the subcontinent.

The most important of these is the frightening increase in population. When the British left in 1947 there were approximately three hundred million people in India and thirty million in Pakistan. The population of India has grown three-fold and that of Pakistan five-fold. The combined population of South Asia today stands at nearly 1.5 billion inhabitants, more than that of China. Because of lack of education and population stabilisation measures absolute poverty is on the increase, linked to a steady increase in population. This, in turn, has led to degradation of the environment, deterioration in sanitary conditions, pollution of the water bodies and atmosphere, contamination of ground water, and soil depletion. In Bangladesh much of the ground water is contaminated by arsenic. Consequences of global warming will be increasingly felt in South Asia with the rise in levels of ocean waters. In Pakistan advancing desert like conditions are being experienced.

Pakistan's present difficulties, as in the case of many other developing countries, stem from neglect of the social sector over a long period of time. Pakistan's defence expenditure as percentage of total expenditure has been hovering around twenty five percent since about 1980. Paradoxically, in spite of the reduction of the external threat, Pakistan's sense of insecurity has actually deepened. Drug trafficking, increasing societal violence, terrorism and sectarianism linked to the spread of small arms have all contributed to the insecurity. The Pakistan military hierarchy as also the better off segments of Pakistan society are now unsure about the states' ability to prevent further inroads by the radical groups. They fear it could lead to creeping *talibanisation* of Pakistan. They are aware that the superior firepower of the Pakistan army might not count for very much for stemming the onslaught of motivated *jehadi* fighters in urban surroundings should they infiltrate in larger numbers from Afghanistan to Pakistan for helping their counterparts in Pakistan to take over the country. By pushing itself to the forefront during the formative stages of the movement for introduction of radical Islam into Pakistan society the Pakistan military did not anticipate the quagmire into which it was plunging when it assumed the responsibility of becoming the guardian of the Islamic ideological identity. In the initial stages the exercise was undertaken more from the point of view of strengthening the military's position vis-à-vis the political dispensation than from any special leaning toward Islamic purity. The difference being that after having continued the pretence for nearly twenty years the Pakistan military has virtually cut off its escape routes.

The proliferation of small arms is a matter of immediate concern to the nations of the subcontinent. Democracy in the majority of the countries of the Third World or the world that became independent in the second half of the 20th century has yet to take effective root. In all such societies where democracy is not present, or is ineffective, large sections of the people who feel marginalised are increasingly taking recourse to the bullet as a viable alternative to the ballot. Even in countries where democracy has taken root there still remain large tracts where there is an increasing demand for small arms. It is axiomatic that where there is a persistent demand supply channels would get established, one way or the other. The point that gets highlighted is that it is the failure of the state, more than anything else, that is responsible for the increase in demand for small arms from otherwise law abiding elements: for self-protection, for keeping at bay the henchmen of political parties who have started playing an extortionist role, and for warding off so many other types of threats which the state is unable to deal with in an effective manner. (The situation in the tribal areas of NWFP, Baluchistan and elsewhere, where the gun culture is a way of life for the people of the region is different; there it is the proliferation of the more lethal variety of small arms that is cause for concern).

In fact, it would not be an exaggeration to state that in many countries - and several provinces in those countries can be singled out for special mention – the state itself, or its instrumentalities are seen to pose the biggest threat to the people's well being. Bloated and corrupt bureaucracies, rapacious law and order forces and the venal political class have all combined to make the people bereft of hope for sustenance, or justice. Should this trend continue small arms proliferation is likely to go up in Pakistan by a factor of five, ten or twenty in the coming years. Hence, the most efficacious response to small arms proliferation remains the establishment of 'good governance'; or the restoration of effective governance where the state exists only in name or in the guise of uniformed instruments of brutality. It is not the intent here to single out Pakistan in this regard. The state of affairs just described exists across the board, to a greater or lesser degree, in most countries where small arms proliferation is taking place.

The most ineffectively governed states and, at the other end, the most repressive states, are likely to face greater violence through an increasing reliance on the gun culture due to the criminal intimidation of the populace linked to political 'warlordism' raising its ugly head. In Pakistan the religious militias have, to a large extent, taken over this role. A connected phenomenon that has a bearing on the subject is the 'ghettoisation' of the elite – the political elite and the moneyed classes. In earlier times it used to be the 'have nots' who generally remained restricted to limited spaces called ghettos while the better off classes had the run of the place, the freedom to go almost anywhere without let or hindrance. What is seen in the present times is a grand reversal of what went before. That is to say, it is now the political elite and the big 'haves' who have become restricted to specific areas of cities, to their 'guilded ghettos' which, in a manner of speaking, remain ghettos no matter how beautiful the mansions or how manicured the lawns. Owing to the breakdown of the social cohesion of societies, these privileged elements no longer enjoy the freedom to wander about wherever they like.

It is this stratum of society – the privileged elite – that is equally to be held responsible for the spread of small arms. The reason being that they are unwilling, or unable, to move about freely without heavily armed escorts. When the most privileged and at least hypothetically the most secure element of any society 'demands' sophisticated weapons for its own protection by way of large security escorts they automatically induce waves of menace in their wake for the ordinary people as they move about. Since the upper echelons of any society are deemed to be the trendsetters it would only be a matter of time before other people start emulating this trend. What is true at the unit level – the unit being a town, province or state – is equally true at the global level. In the latter case the most secure nations of the world keep adding to their security, while the least secure can only hope for a more rational world order to emerge to bail them out. The important issue that needs to be understood is that, as in the case of nuclear weapons, so also in the case of small arms, the vertical proliferation is way beyond the horizontal proliferation that is taking place.

It is well appreciated that there is an increasing threat of terrorism around the world. But it is invariably the ordinary people who – being wholly dependent on the state for their security – bear the brunt of terrorist attacks. Should the state not afford adequate protection, sophisticated small arms will continue to proliferate. In many cities around the world the police are abandoning large sectors of the city where the dregs of society live or where immigrant communities live, to criminal gangs who terrorise the people living there. Tacit understanding between the police and the local gangs, who are expected to limit their operations to such areas, leave the people living there at the mercy of the local thugs. Here again, the day is not far off before newer groups acquire small arms to protect themselves. When the state fails to provide protection the people feel obliged to look elsewhere.

The next major causative factor for the increasing ungovernability of Pakistan – to some extent other countries of the subcontinent as well - is the horrendous population growth and the concomitant destruction of the natural environment. This, in itself, becomes sufficient cause for societal violence and the spread of small arms. For, had the population of the subcontinent, which was around eight hundred million plus at the beginning of the nineteen eighties decade, stabilised at around that figure or even at a slightly higher level, many of the intractable problems that these nations face today, especially increased societal violence, would not have been there, or even if they had manifested themselves they would not have seemed intractable. The corollary to this statement would also hold good. Should Pakistan's population double in the next twenty to thirty years as it is bound to do at the present growth rate, governing Pakistan could become a near impossibility, irrespective of the form of government in place. In fact the veneer of civilisation would have disappeared from large swathes of Pakistan and the subcontinent, north of the Vindhyas.

Today the subcontinent has reached such a stage of overpopulation that should it become technically feasible to project ten thousand people every day to a colony on the moon or Mars it would not make a dent in the population growth rate or lead to an improvement in livability in most parts. Cities bursting at the seams with the deprived segments still continuing to proliferate is a dimension of the problem that has not received sufficient attention in Pakistan or a purposeful move towards its tackling. It is leading to a lowered quality of life for the majority of the inhabitants and results in further breakdown of the social cohesion of society. If it remains unchecked it will lead to greater societal violence and sectarian conflicts as the resource base shrinks. The need to kill the others will no longer be met by the simpler variety of small arms being used today in Karachi and elsewhere in Pakistan. The USA and the West have been blamed for their policies, perhaps rightly so, for the increasing marginalisation of the populations in developing countries. Whatever be the case, unless population stabilisation is achieved in these countries incomes redistribution, should it take place, would not be able to solve their problems.

In an interesting meeting that the Pakistan president is reported to have had with The IndUS Entrepreneurs (TIE), the former was apparently jolted to learn that Pakistan is 10-20 years behind India in Information Technology. In the same meeting TIE referred to the General having told *Newsweek* that "only 10 per cent of Pakistanis are *jehadis*". When it was pointed out to him that 10 per cent meant 15 million *jehadis* the General claimed to have been misquoted and amended the figure to 1 per cent or 1.5 million *jehadis*.[4] While the Pakistani head glibly changed the decimal point by bringing down the figure from 15 million to 1.5 million, he had unwittingly given the game away. The Pakistan government is itself not too sure as to the correct figure and even if one takes the figure to be somewhere in between the two figures mentioned it still implies that radical Islam has proliferated extensively due to state patronage extended to it by short-sighted policies of the different Pakistan governments coming after General Zia-ul-Haq. The more worrisome aspect for Pakistan should be the fact that, whichever way one looks at it, the *jehadis* outnumber the Pakistan military by a ratio that could vary from 3:1 to perhaps 20:1. To this significant disparity must be added the number of supporters in the army itself who are silent backers of the radical Islamists. As if this were not grim enough note has also to be taken of the potential of the withdrawing Taliban from Afghanistan and the cadres trained by Osama Bin Laden to reinforce the *jehadi* elements in Pakistan.

Besides the Pakistan government the people of Pakistan themselves are following an ostrich-like policy by ignoring the gravity of the threat posed to their way of life, lived over the centuries, by the new Taliban type Islamic dispensation. Stupidly, and short-sightedly they keep on claiming that such radicalism represents a threat to India when, in actual fact, they have simply not mobilised themselves to face the challenge squarely. India would certainly be threatened by Pakistan going under in this manner. However, India has already been facing the hostility of the Pakistan military for over 50 years. Obviously, the nuclear threat remains a constant; whether nuclear blackmail, or the ultimate launch madness, were it to be indulged in by the military itself, or the military-mullah combine, or the radical Islamists on their own. Additionally, as opposed to the situation in the second half of the 20th century, most of the countries that are today dominant in the world support India in this regard.

The attention of the world is suddenly focused on Pakistan, not as the people of Pakistan have been led to believe as a frontline state for the 'Battle of Afghanistan', but as a prelude to the 'Battle for Pakistan' that must surely follow, irrespective of the outcome in Afghanistan. The US led coalition may not at the moment feel that the situation might be as grim as in Afghanistan. It would yet be mindful of recent history in this regard - i.e., the sudden collapse of the USSR, the fall of the Berlin Wall, the fall of Saigon and the return of the Ayatollah to Iran.

The Pakistani generals are not making much headway in tackling the *jehadi* elements in Pakistan. Every now and then they carry out swoops to round up men belonging to various organisations and ban their activities relating to the collection of funds. These non-serious attempts that are never carried through to their logical conclusion are made every now and then just for effect to placate the

Americans or feeble attempts to create a more favourable atmosphere for talks with the Indian government, should it become necessary. It is possible that the generals, alarmed at their growth, are trying to take the measure of the radical Islamic groups. Every time they talked tough they had been forced to retreat ignominiously because they did not have the stomach to enforce the tough measures announced with much fanfare. Many among the top brass of the military hierarchy have realised that the *jehadi* groups need to be controlled before they become strong enough to give battle to the military, should they feel impelled to do so. The reason why the military is reluctant to go all the way to effectively curb them has not so much to do with Kashmir as is being made out to be the case; for the truth is that the *jehadis* now are a bigger challenge to the Pakistan army than the Indian army in Kashmir. The Pakistan military is reluctant to go after the radical Islamists because it is not sure whether the instrumentalities – the rank and file of the army and the ISI - with which they intend to deal with the radical groups will carry out their orders.

A radical structural change is being initiated in Pakistan through the militarisation of Islam. The marginalisation of the polity by the military, as much out of pique as anything else, after the Kargil misadventure resulted in the strengthening of the radical Islamic elements at the cost of the political classes. To say that the space being vacated by the political parties due to military action would lead to strengthening the military would be incorrect. The military always had it within its power to usurp the levers of power whenever they chose to do so. It did not lead to civil war in the west as happened in the erstwhile province of East Pakistan, now Bangladesh. Public protests were tolerated up to a point, but dealt firmly when they threatened to get out of hand. The independence of the media could never be sustained for any length of time. Their criticism of the military has generally been muted. It was never allowed to go beyond the restraints set by the authorities to become a sustained campaign for ouster of the military regimes.

The people of Pakistan must appreciate that the earlier cycles of military rule followed by civil unrest leading to re-establishment of civilian governments may no longer apply in Pakistan in the future. The earlier patterns of alternating military rule followed by 'imposed' civilian rule by sufferance of the military may have changed. The situation obtaining after the present military take-over stands radically altered. For one thing, the political class is now being marginalised in its entirety, in order to consolidate and perpetuate the military regime. Therefore, in destroying the legitimacy of the political class and the space ceded to the political process from time to time the stakes have become enormous. The political class may henceforth be obliged to exploit other possibilities never considered before to not only incommode, but to push out the military for once and for all. The reverse of what the military is intending to do to them. Threatened with extinction the politicians could even start mobilising their not inconsiderable resources for covert actions against the military, unlike the earlier occasions. Secondly, since there is an inherent opposition to all forms of authoritarianism the populace, not having legitimate political outlets may now be obliged to coalesce around the militant groups since they remain the only cohesive structure capable of mounting a challenge to the military, at whatever stage they feel strong enough to do so. Hence, Pakistan may have to pay dearly for demolishing the political classes so comprehensively and thereby allowing the political space to be taken over by radical Islamist groups for whom dialogue and compromise represent alien concepts.

The other reason for the situation becoming more volatile and potentially more grave than in the past 50 years is the fact that after centuries the Muslim clergy sense an opening for grabbing political power, not as an appendage to a political party or some other governance fraternity, but directly in their own right as in the case of Iran. Pakistan has not yet reached the stage where take-over by the Muslim clergy is round the corner. Should, however, the military not restore the political process the chances of Pakistan too coming under the heel of the Islamic orthodoxy could become greater than would have been possible in earlier times.

India's ancient culture, wisdom and lore will continue to attract people from around the world. Pakistan, with its negativism, has no such attraction for anybody outside Pakistan. Since it has built itself exclusively around Islam, outsiders can easily find Islamic culture and tradition at its source or in a dozen or more Islamic countries. Unless Pakistan changes course it will mortgage its future; because hatred and animosity towards the country that had nurtured Islam in its bosom for a full thousand years cannot be the basis for any edifice built on humanistic foundations. Pakistan's uniqueness, in this day and age, lies in its ability to attract elements at the Islamic fringe, who come only to learn the terrorist trade; the source that corrupts the mind and corrodes the heart.

It is difficult to hazard a guess as to which route Pakistan will take in the coming years in its quest for self-definition. Empirical evidence suggests that the path of military ascendancy which was directly responsible for the military confrontations of the past cannot lead the country towards any worthwhile goals, for Pakistan as a nation or for the people of Pakistan as a social grouping. The latest military coup, travelling the well-trodden path of the earlier military dictators merely confirms for the majority of the Pakistan people and the world at large their belief that having become addicted to absolutism for so long the Pakistan military finds it difficult to remain in the barracks or to keep its hands off the coffers of the state. For, at the end of the day, it is largely the military that has bankrupted Pakistan through their unaffordable arsenals and unproductive wars against India.

The Pakistan military establishment had a field day for most of the 1980s and 1990s when they were able to convince the world that unless they were allowed to go their way, they would not be able to deliver. Not being able to deliver in the Cold War era referred to the pushing back of the Soviet forces from Afghanistan by means of the forays launched from Mujahideen bases in NWFP and elsewhere in Pakistan. At that time, led by the CIA, the US establishment was willing to go along, turning a blind eye to several parallel developments not really to their liking. Having perfected the policy of extracting maximum benefits from their backers the Pakistan generals continued to refine the tried and tested methods even after the collapse of the Soviet empire. Glibly overlooking the fact that the Taliban were nurtured in Pakistan and supported by the Pakistan army and ISI these generals now plead before the world, and lately with the Indian leaders, that unless they are backed they will not be able to control the Taliban or prevent the creeping *jehadisation* of Pakistan society. In fact, some had even felt emboldened to say that they would not be able to guarantee the safety of the nuclear weapons, or from their falling into the wrong hands. These excuses now ring hollow. September 11 changed the tenor of the nuclear blackmail tune the generals were fond of playing to the world.

By themselves militant Islamist elements or, for that matter, the radical elements from any other religion would never have been in a position to establish themselves politically anywhere on the subcontinent if they had not been given a leg up by the military regimes in Pakistan or the political parties in the subcontinent. In some respects, the political parties became their own worst enemies when they first allowed elements with criminal backgrounds to contest elections on their party tickets, the sole criterion being 'winability' and nothing else. The political parties did so for short-term gains, thinking that once elected they would be able to control such elements. They were unable to do so. Over a period of time the criminal elements used their newfound political clout to further consolidate their hold by checkmating the police. Muscle and money power got augmented to the extent that soon enough they were able to get themselves elected in their own right; even playing off the political parties against each other or excluding them from their fiefdoms unless they withdrew or diluted the criminal cases against them. In the same manner fundamentalist elements, especially in Pakistan and Bangladesh, managed to get electoral footholds through alliance with political parties seeking to expand their vote base. Not unsurprisingly there was a price to be paid for supping with the devil. There is always a price to be paid for supping with the devil.

    Having got a foothold the criminal-fundamentalist elements, being better organised than some of the political parties on the subcontinent, went on to quickly expand their base at the cost of their benefactors – in Pakistan, the military as well as the political parties. That was not all. Funding patterns underwent change with the flow of money raised from narcotics, gun running and the flesh trade, activities that generally go hand in hand. The underground or parallel economy of Pakistan expanded further. It found channels for turning black money into white. At the end of the day the situation obtaining reveals the criminalisation of politics, the politicalisation of crime and the syndicalisation of the crime mafias and radical Islamic groups; with significant build up of warlike capabilities – arms, men and money – to wage terror within the country as also across national frontiers. In the process they built up the capacity to challenge the state's monopoly on violence, an essential attribute of state sovereignty. In fact, they have possibly gathered the critical mass to withstand any urge that the military may develop to dismantle their bases or to undermine their strength. They have acquired the manpower strength, the weapons strength, the ideological base and adequate financial muscle to meet the military's challenge.

The Pakistan military has often intervened in the democratic process by accusing the civilian governments, normally established at its behest, of mismanagement and rampant corruption. While this may have been true in almost all cases the fact remains that unless sufficient time is allowed to the political process to right itself, or cleanse itself democratically, the process (of governance) gets further degraded due to absolutist type interventions. The military had accused the political class of having siphoned off funds worth US $100 billion and parked them in safe havens outside the country. It is not inconceivable that the political class, if given the unfettered right to investigate the military hierarchy, would be able to come up with a figure which would be significantly higher in the case of fortunes amassed by military generals and their families over the last fifty years. It becomes plausible to believe in the higher rake-offs by the military because of the exceptionally high military spending when taken as a percentage of the GDP or the annual state budget. It needs to be added that the military spending and defence deals hardly ever came under expert civilian scrutiny. Therefore, to say the least, under normal circumstances the Pakistan military hierarchy should be the last set of people to be casting aspersions on others on this count. In touching upon this aspect of corruption by the political class and the military the moneys derived by some of the latter through linkage with narcotics mafias and gun running has not been taken into account. Should the latter be taken into account the sums arrived at would be astronomical, even by global standards. The Bank of Credit and Commerce International (BCCI) case highlighted the patronage provided by the military hierarchy to criminal activities having international ramifications.

Deconstruction of the existing state in Pakistan becomes necessary for several reasons, all of them attributable to the military establishment in one way or another. The first reason is the acquisition of nuclear weapons by the Pakistan state with the attendant risk of transfer of nuclear materials to other states and non-state actors. It would be recalled that from the very inception Pakistan had to an extent mortgaged its nuclear programme to outside financiers, notably Libya and Saudi Arabia to raise the funds necessary for establishing the nuclear development infrastructure. Many times during its chequered history the programme had been referred to glowingly as the 'Islamic bomb'. Therefore, well before the advent of the radical Islamists as a potent force in Pakistan the rites of passage of the Islamic bomb had been set in motion.

The second reason for the deconstruction of the Pakistan state in its present form relates to the creeping *jehadisation* of Pakistan society, mostly through coercion and violence and through the receipt of funds from outside Pakistan. The funds for pushing the agenda of radical Islam came from Saudi Arabia in its incipient phase. More recently these have been augmented by funds channelled to these groups from the proceeds of drug trafficking. Both of the reasons outlined for deconstruction would have sufficed even when taken singly. Together they add up to a major threat to the well being of Pakistan society, India and the subcontinent and with each passing year a credible threat in being to global society. Methodologies for controlled deconstruction of the Pakistan state can be considered in any of the following ways:

- Restructuring Pakistan society in a credible manner to eliminate the threat.
- A major initiative along the same lines by India for organising and supporting the elements that wish to oppose the challenge posed to their life and liberty by radical Islamists.
- Deconstruction engineered by the global community.

The uncontrolled deconstruction of Pakistan could proceed along any of the following lines:

- *Talibanisation* of Pakistan with military acquiescence, but without direct military involvement.
- *Talibanisation* of the military leading to take over by the *jehadis*.
- Development of fault lines, leading to confrontation between elements demanding complete Islamisation and status quo-ists.
- Polarisation between the military-*jehadi* combine and the political parties demanding restoration of democracy.
- Vertical split in the military between radical Islamists and moderates.
- Break up of Pakistan by the cutting loose of Baluchistan and Sindh.

- Break up of Pakistan resulting from major military reverses with India.
- Break up of Pakistan engineered by India with support from the global community.
- Annihilation of Pakistan as a result of nuclear exchange with India.

The *talibanisation* of Pakistan along the lines that radical Islam is being imposed in Afghanistan is not a prospect that brings cheer to the average Pakistan citizen, the Pakistan diaspora, India, Iran, Central Asian Republics, the nations of the Middle East as presently constituted, its great benefactor China, or the world at large. The military dispensation that runs Pakistan being aware of the global antipathy toward an outcome of this nature shrewdly exploits the global concern, more so of the Indian leaders. Since the prospect of a Taliban type take-over directly or in a power sharing arrangement with the military is no longer as remote as it was a few years ago it would be prudent to have a closer look at the situation as it obtains today in Pakistan in this regard.

There is no doubt that radical Islam has taken firm root in Pakistan in the last two decades since the *madrasa* culture was given a fillip by an earlier military regime. While it would be difficult to hazard a guess as to the actual numbers involved it can be estimated that including its supporters in the military the number of sympathisers could be reckoned in millions. As a percentage of the population of Pakistan this figure could be anything between ten to twenty percent. Of this figure the hard core of supporters would perhaps be a few hundred thousand. The number that has actually undergone military training or would be capable of bearing arms would perhaps be around hundred thousand if added to the elements exfiltrating from Afghanistan. What needs to be taken note of is that with the increase in the number of *madrasas* and the rate at which the population is proliferating in the absence of modern education and dynamic family welfare programmes the absolute number of adherents of radical Islam could keep increasing significantly from year to year. Should the trend not be reversed by the Pakistan government, or the political classes, it would be possible for the radical Islamist groups to increase their electoral representation manifold and demand a major share in governance. In all the elections held so far the number of seats obtained by the radical groups has been insignificant. This was one of the reasons for the political parties and the ruling classes to discount the threat and even indulge these elements from time to time. What the people opposed to a state take-over by these elements do not appreciate is that the radical Islamist groups have in the interim augmented their resources in arms, funds and followers very significantly and could conceivably spring a major surprise at the hustings with a shrewd admix of muscle and money power with tacit backing from supporters in the Pakistan military.

Taking off from the situation as it currently obtains in Pakistan, related also to the dominant geo-political equations in and around the subcontinent, it should be possible to hazard a guess as to the politico-military trends in Pakistan in the years ahead. In order of the probability of their occurrence in the next two to five years, possibly a bit beyond, these are likely to be:

- The present military dictatorship, assisted by USA, strengthens its hold on power and brings in some form of guided democracy.
- In spite of their present state of emasculation the political parties re-gather their strength and mount an effective challenge to displace the military.

- The military and the mullahs jointly strengthen their hold on Pakistan in an informal power sharing arrangement.
- The military feel obliged to cut the Islamist radical groups down to size.
- The Islamist militant groups forge a strategic alliance – possibly with the Taliban elements who might have gone underground in Afghanistan as well - to challenge the military's dominance; forcing them to yield ground to an Islamic dispensation.
- The emergence of other centres of counter violence.
- The reemergence of the Taliban regime in parts of Afghanistan as the king maker in Pakistan (after a protracted guerrilla struggle against US intervention).
- Rebellions in Sindh, Baluchistan and elsewhere.
- Any other permutation and combination depending upon the relative strength of the wielders, or potential wielders, of power in Pakistan.
- The re-emergence of MQM as the dominant force in Karachi.

The (plausible) scenarios listed above for Pakistan in the ensuing decade represent an array of probable outcomes. While the relative strengths of the contenders can be assessed with reasonable accuracy at this point in time the same strengths may vary in as little as two to three years down the line. Much will depend upon the externalities that impinge on the course of events in Pakistan, India and the subcontinent.

Since Pakistan has centred its existence around confrontation with India it would follow that any increase in India's economic strength and ability to deal with the low intensity conflict and cross-border terrorism sponsored by Pakistan will impact heavily on Pakistan's internal condition. China, while continuing to back Pakistan could have misgivings after the US intervention. Its support, though seemingly enduring, will itself be contingent upon the progress of the US intervention in Afghanistan, Pakistan and Central Asia. The strengthening of Indo-US relations could be further influenced as much by China's geo-political strategy in Asia and the transfer of nuclear materials and missiles technologies; which are likely to be viewed far more seriously in the future than was the case in the earlier decade.

Pakistan is beholden to China in more ways than one. It has ceded territory of the erstwhile state of Jammu and Kashmir under its occupation in Gilgit and Baltistan to China when it had no legal right to do so. All actions relating to China taken by Pakistan have almost entirely been on the basis of its hostility toward India. This hostility has brought upon the Pakistan rulers over the years a blinkered vision that prevented them from seeing the bigger picture in the longer-term horizon of the coming decades of the 21st century. By not reaching accommodations with India on the larger issues that go well beyond Kashmir when looking at the future of the subcontinent it has deprived itself, India and all the countries of the subcontinent with openings into Central Asia and beyond that could have enormously benefited the subcontinent as a whole.

In the process it had given China a free hand to do what it liked in Central Asia. Had China consolidated its economic hold on the Central Asian Republics and built the rail and road communications through China to the Pacific Ocean, Pakistan's importance for the Central Asian Republics would have diminished. Pakistan, while not being unimportant as a fellow Islamic country, looked attractive as a route to the vast markets of the subcontinent. Hence, viewed from the long-term geo-economic viability of the subcontinent in the global perspective of the unfolding century Pakistan, it turns out, has undermined itself as much, if not more than it has India. Should it persist with its confrontationist path it will further compromise its economic future. It must realise that it can hurt India by denying it access to Central Asia up to a point. India has the size as well as the large internal market to guarantee its economic viability and remain attractive to the rest of the world as a trading partner. Pakistan could literally wither away economically.

There are three distinct ways of looking at the all round decline that is manifestly taking place in Pakistan; subjectively from within Pakistan; a little more objectively from India; and from a global perspective. Taking first of all the Pakistan scene as perceived from within by its inhabitants it becomes evident that the situation appears different when viewed from the Punjab heartland or through the mindset of the Pakistan war machine, which has been the true power centre of governance, for well nigh five decades. The latter have added to their strength by providing themselves with reckonable grass roots support through the increasing membership of the radical Islamic groups that were created, armed and funded by them. For the best part of the twenty years since their inception they were generally kept on a tight leash by the military intelligence services of Pakistan. This could change. For this group i.e. the military and the radical Islamists with their backers the road to resurrection apparently lies in greater militancy, and greater Islamisation of the nation. Some would call it a blinkered vision, while they themselves would be inclined to term it as a continuation of the struggle that had gone before. These elements constituting the virulent and violent segment of the state have nearly always been able to influence domestic and foreign policy through their armed strength and cohesion. By their constitution and upbringing they are prone to violence. What they lack by way of popular mandate they make up through their stranglehold on the levers of state power and, more recently, through the *jehadi* legions that they are creating.

The second important group that tacitly backed the Pakistan establishment right from the inception of Pakistan were the landed gentry and the big business groups who controlled the private wealth in Pakistan. Not willing to see any diminution in their privileges or property they gradually started co-opting the upper echelons of the military and the civil services into their fold. The latter hardly needed coaxing. In spite of their smallness in numbers there could not have been significant erosion in their power and their holdings on account of their solid links, both within Pakistan as well as trans national. While their support to the governing elites never wavered all this time they have now started entertaining certain doubts on the viability of the Pakistan state as also the increasing Islamisation of the country which they feel might, if it is not moderated in time, one day attempt to question their present life style and supposedly un-Islamic ways. Because of this anxiety they have redeployed a significant portion of their wealth in safer havens where they and their progeny could continue to enjoy their wealth should, at any stage, things become too hot for them in Pakistan.

What applies to the powerful old moneyed elite of Pakistan applies equally to the new robber barons, namely, the political elite, the military-civil elite which traditionally has been heading the large public sector corporations, and the latest – perhaps the most powerful – entrant, the narco – crime syndicates. Almost each and everyone of them have salted wealth away from their own country to provide themselves financial security should the state of Pakistan decay beyond redemption, or for the eventuality of the Islamic dispensation taking over at any stage. What these people or classes have realised is that their tolerance and support of the radical Islamists to keep them off their backs merely strengthened the latter. They get emboldened and demand greater radicalisation and participation in governance, till the time comes when they have gathered sufficient mass to make a direct bid for seizing power; by challenging the state through violence, or by leveraging the state machinery to enhance their prospects, whenever elections are held. The radical Islam factions are shrewd enough to know that, on their own, their chances for coming to power through legitimate means remain slim. Hence, while in the shorter time horizon the military dispensations and, for that matter, any other dispensation running the country derives 'some' strength from the backing given by fundamentalists, in the longer term it is the fundamentalists who are the ultimate gainers. They would have piggy-backed themselves to state power.

In the light of the foregoing the hypocrisy of the Pakistani ruling elite comes out clearly. To take an example, neither the generals running the country nor the politicians and certainly not the wealthy classes would be willing to countenance an abridgement of their own liberal and effete life style. They would not be willing to allow their women folk to be circumscribed by the veil. Neither they nor their women would like to be confined to the four walls of the house and follow the barbaric codes being applied to the women in Afghanistan. Since such a possibility cannot be discounted it becomes incomprehensible to fathom as to why the people who have ruled Pakistan in various combinations (among themselves) are allowing the menace of radical Islam to grow. Because there can be no doubt that, going by the past practices of almost all the earlier revolutions of this type in many countries, the first set of people who are beheaded, incarcerated, and whose properties are confiscated have invariably been the ruling and the privileged elite of the former regimes. Neither the past leaders nor the present leaders of Pakistan, including their immediate circles, would like to see their own women mistreated. Since, at various points in time they have been instrumental in supporting and strengthening the elements who could, if they came to power, stifle the women and liberal elements, as also the intellectuals in Pakistan, it is high time that they faced up to their culpability and started taking effective steps to first check and then marginalise the radical Islamic elements. Running away from it all when the day of reckoning comes would hardly be the response that the other Pakistanis, who too would not like to be ruled by the radical Islamists, would expect of them. They played their part in leading the country into the quagmire in which it finds itself. They must find a way out before all ways are blocked for them.

Radical groups in Pakistan have been advocating *jehad* for breaking up India. Many in the military would be hoping for the same to come to pass. What these elements fail to realise is that no matter how much the Pakistani establishment, the ISI, or the militant groups try to foment unrest by targeting disgruntled fellow Islamists in India, they are hardly likely to make much headway. While seemingly flailing as a democracy due to political chicanery and regional pulls, India at every level, has achieved a cohesiveness that brings all elements together whenever there is a grave threat to the security of the country. This has been amply demonstrated time and again. It has strengthened its cohesion in several other fields, not apparent to people dependent for their inputs solely on the media. For all its failings it is a vibrant democracy. India is an amazing democratic experiment. Perhaps no other country, comparable in size and diversity to India, could have carried forward the democratic experiment with such élan, possibly too much élan. Zulfiqar Ali Bhutto, in a moment of churlish eloquence referred to it as, 'the noise and chaos of Indian democracy'. Truly, the noise, chaos, unruliness and infighting drown out the real strengths that have built up. In the ultimate test of a democracy, what is sought to be established is that the voice of the people should be the sole criterion for transference of power to elected governments, whenever elections are ahead. By that criterion India comes out a winner every time. Notwithstanding the killings, turbulence and rigging that take place during the elections, transfer of power, both at the centre and the states, automatically takes place in conformity with the election result. There have been no exceptions to this rule, despite the frequency of elections brought on by unstable coalition politics. Whatever the comments and criticism, the decision of the President of India when he invites elected leaders of political parties to form a government, is respected.

In short, democracy in India has come to stay. It is not easy to destabilise democracies the size of India where governments of different hues keep being formed with changing coalition partners. The electorate, though largely illiterate, has been smartly punishing governments with large governing majorities with near complete decimation when they betrayed the confidence of the people. This happened to Mrs. Indira Gandhi, perhaps the strongest prime minister in post-independence India. It happened, thereafter, to Rajiv Gandhi, her son who had been given the largest plurality after his mother's death. The Indian electorate threw him out of office when he was caught up in a financial scandal. Functioning democracies provide safety valves to all segments of society.

India has another advantage in its democratic set up that provides stability of a type that Pakistan lacks; and ordinarily can never hope to achieve unless it restructures itself in the Indian mould. This is explained by the fact that while New Delhi becomes the punching bag for all provincial governments and disgruntled elements, they know in their heart of hearts that ultimately New Delhi and the central government are merely geographic and appellative entities. The government at the centre is merely the sum total of the representatives sent from all over India to the parliament in the capital. No region, ethnic or linguistic group can really dominate everyone else. There is no dominant provincial entity like in the case of the province of Punjab in Pakistan that can relegate the other provinces to an inferior status.

4

Reconstruction

With the dissolution of the British Indian Empire the newly independent states of India and Pakistan inherited a structure comprising a Central Government and provinces with elected legislatures and a measure of autonomy. In Pakistan constitution making was delayed and even when one was completed in 1956 it did not take long for a highly centralised military dictatorship to be established in the country in 1958. It continued for over a decade. The tensions resulting from the agitations to force the military to go back to the barracks were so high that when the hold of the dictatorship ended the country itself broke apart.

The only way the confidence of the people of the different regions can be restored is by conceding maximum provincial autonomy. The Pakistan state, which is still looking for a durable socio-political system, cannot hope to progress without the full support of all the people. Full autonomy could ensure that support. It has to be remembered that a system that has been subverted with such regular frequency cannot suddenly get on to a good start with the restoration of democracy. In Pakistan democracy will have to be nurtured 'de novo' with the assurance that the military will never be able to again overturn the system, regardless of its failings.

While nations of the world have, in their own way, tried to move ahead, some unsuccessfully, in their march to freedom or nationhood in the post-colonial era, Pakistan has managed to go round and round in circles, i.e., military coup followed by a short civilian spell, again a military coup, back to a civilian government and so on. The process has been aptly summed up by a Pakistani journalist, who wrote:

"NO ROAD in Pakistan is more extensively travelled on than the one leading back to democracy. At the same time, no road is more signposted with the crucifixion of hope than this one. It is not in our military coups that we have betrayed ourselves so much as in our return marches to democracy. If every coup has kindled the irrational emotionalism which forms so strong a part of our national character, the aftermath of every coup has gifted us a fresh set of problems, more complicated and intractable than those originally meant to be solved".[5]

One has then to ask oneself whether the military artfully contrives during their various direct interventions to create situations that 'oblige' elected governments to founder!

Pakistan has to restructure its state entity in the light of the changing nature of its threat perceptions, as well as the globalisation that, in some form or another, is forcing changes on almost all countries of the world. Should an objective Pakistani based in Islamabad, Karachi, London or elsewhere question the basic tenets of state security it will be found that the threat perceptions of the 20th century i.e., the first five decades of Pakistan's existence, have altered considerably. To begin with the old Soviet Union, which could threaten Pakistan from the north, has disintegrated; and since China is a close ally of Pakistan there is no military threat to Pakistan from the north, like it might have appeared in an earlier era. Pakistan exercised a high degree of control or influence over the Taliban in Afghanistan before the US intervention. At certain levels that influence would always remain because no Afghan regime would be in a position to remain hostile for long toward Pakistan. India, should Pakistan not interfere in Kashmir, would not pose any threat on account of its ineluctable need to divert maximum resources toward population stabilisation and socio-economic development. For this it needs a prolonged spell of peace. Tensions with India, wherever they obtain and whenever they obtain, are generally instigated by Pakistan, which has been raising the ante from time to time. No doubt, should the cross border terrorism, which Pakistan refers to as *jehad*, cross India's threshold of tolerance then India, most probably, would take recourse to retaliatory punitive strikes of a limited nature. Thereafter, it would be up to Pakistan to prevent further escalation. Hence, as things stand, the escalatory process is in the hands of Pakistan. Should it wish to reduce tensions it is free to do so. It could then concentrate its meagre resources on development in the socio-economic sector rather than the bloated defence sector.

In the light of what has been mentioned above it becomes apparent that should Pakistan enter into a period of further decline, either economic or territorial or both, the blame for it would lie squarely on the shoulders of the Pakistan military establishment. The externalities that impinged on Pakistan's security in the previous years are no longer operative unless Pakistan itself decides to resurrect threats that have virtually disappeared from its military security horizon. The new threats that Pakistan faces are almost entirely of its own making. At the present juncture in order of priority these could be tabulated as: fall out from the situation in Afghanistan; creeping radicalisation of Pakistan; economic decline leading to greater social unrest; support of the withdrawing Taliban to the *jehadi* elements in Pakistan for making a bid to grab political power or to wrest control of the levers of the state by challenging the military, or by subversion of the military.

The time may have come for Pakistan to do a smart about turn on its negotiating strategy with India. Kashmir should be put on the backburner in the next round of talks between the two leaders and progress carried forward on all other issues. Should that happen, an amazing turn around could take place in as little as two to three years. The positive fallout for Pakistan would be: amelioration in its economic situation; greater cultural interflow between the two countries; and remarkable increase in tourism related activities between the two of them, which itself could generate employment for several hundred thousand people and revenues running into hundreds, if not thousand of crores of rupees annually – once these activities pick up.

Dismantling a structure is not a very difficult task. When a structure is terminally weakened it can crumble fast as a result of a strong impact. It would be incorrect at this stage to say that the state of Pakistan is about to crumble. The issue is being raised because the road on which the military government of Pakistan has turned the state leads to terminal decline and nowhere else. If Pakistan continues along this route the final collapse could come about any time. It would be recalled that not only the Soviet government, the whole world was taken aback by the swiftness of the collapse of the Soviet Union. The surprising part is that this collapse did not take place on account of a military reverse or rebellions in the republics. It collapsed, almost overnight, due to the pressure that had been building up within the state while the façade remained intact for the outside observer. It is for the average citizen of Pakistan to take note of the situation and decide for himself (or herself) whether the direction in which the state is headed leads to a rosy, harmonious future or whether it presages the arrival of the darkest period in its short history. That the country must live in harmony with its neighbours and, most importantly India, is on account of the fact that while Pakistan's rulers might wish to turn their back upon the history of their forebears they cannot possibly do the same with the country's geography, no matter how hard they try. It is well known that they have been running hither and thither to align themselves with countries outside their neighbourhood. Unfortunately, this has served only to skewer their perspective. Except for the military establishment the benefits for the people of Pakistan have been illusory.

Should the people of Pakistan, in their wisdom, come round to the view that the governance of Pakistan in the last 50 years has only created an unholy mess which can only become more unholy they must then give a thought to the manner in which they could reconstruct their state. Several pathways that represent a favourable turn of events need to be urgently examined, seriously debated, and efforts made toward their fruition.

Since globalisation is a process that has overtaken the world and cannot be wished away by nations that are already intricately linked into the global economy, it would be prudent to assume that any reconstruction process that helps in the establishment of a healthy democratic tradition should be generally welcomed or acceptable as an alternative. The most likely reconstruction pathways to be considered are:

- Restoration of democracy in concert with the military establishment as a harmonious and irreversible process.
- Reconstruction for a stable democratic order brought on by unmanageable civil unrest forcing the army back into the barracks.

- Reconstruction mandated by the global community in the face of increasing global threat from radical Islamist groups.
- Reconstruction aided by the global community after military intervention by India.
- Reconstruction mandated by the global community due to total economic collapse.
- Reconstruction after a full-scale civil war.
- Reconstruction after the breakaway of one or more of the provinces of Pakistan.

The Turkish Model – How Relevant Is It?

Many in Pakistan have voiced the opinion that a military dictator would be preferable to the rot induced by the politicians. The sentiment has been occasionally voiced outside Pakistan -mainly by Muslims. There are several reasons for this. The first, and foremost, being that subconsciously they may be influenced by the pattern of governments in almost all the countries where Islam holds sway. Democracy, in its true sense, has not taken root in any of the Muslim countries. In the case of Pakistan, the de Gaulle and Kemal Attaturk models do not really apply. The present incumbent is the fourth army chief to seize state power. In at least two of the cases, those of Ayub Khan and Zia-ul-Haq, the process of consolidation, followed by public disillusionment, lasted a full decade before mounting unrest and a mysterious accident forced the reversion to civilian rule, no matter how temporary. Secondly, the circumstances of Kemal Attaturk coming to power in Turkey after the First World War and de Gaulle in France not very much after the Second World War were entirely different. Both these were figures that had achieved near legendary national stature 'prior' to the assumption of the highest office in the land. Not through usurpations of the type perfected by Pakistan army chiefs from time to time.

The state that Pakistan is in today has resulted directly from military interventions in the internal affairs of the country and not entirely on account of the inability of politicians to run the country. They were never really given a chance to do so for any reckonable period of time, seeing the situation in the country when they assumed power. For full fifty years the dominant power in Pakistan has been the military. Military generals have ruled the roost, directly or by proxy, during this entire period, in one form or another. It is they who have brought Pakistan to a state of near terminal degeneration. Hence, to compare the military rulers of Pakistan with de Gaulle or Kemal Attaturk would be a travesty of history and an insult to their memory and the peoples whom they governed.

If Pakistan is now looked upon as an unsafe country where world monetary interests are unwilling to invest the blame can be put squarely on the Pakistan military for having raised the spectre of Islamic fundamentalism and for having bankrupted the public exchequer by cornering the wealth of Pakistan; for sustaining themselves and their single point agenda of engendering hatred towards India. In the process they created psychological distortions for vast segments of Pakistan and Afghan society and pushed them into an area of medieval darkness. To any objective observer of the scene it would become obvious that the only way to push Pakistan over the brink would be to continue with the policy of more of the same i.e. India baiting, India hating.

Post- September 11, a few basic aspects that need to be understood in the reconstruction of Pakistan relate to:

(a) The web of clandestine activity that links the ISI and organisations started by Osama bin Laden is so intricate that to dismantle one automatically involves the other.

(b) The source of all the trouble after the Soviet withdrawal having been Pakistan, no lasting solution for peace in Afghanistan can be found without some restructuring in Pakistan. Unless the latter is also addressed it merely postpones the resolution of the problem; which could emerge in a more virulent form a few years later.

Short sighted - and short-term - agreements reached with the Pakistan military to meet immediate US goals should be replaced by long-term agreements that are manifestly in the interest of the people of Pakistan as well as the comity of nations. These include:

- Closing down of *deeni madaris* in Pakistan.
- De-indoctrination programme.
- Restructuring/modernising of education.
- Spread of IT culture.
- Health package.
- Revitalisation of economy.
- Restoration of democracy in a phased manner with full safeguards.
- Extinguishment of WMD capability.
- Debt rescheduling and financial aid to be linked to progress on the above issues.

Singapore's Senior Minister, Mr. Lee Kuan Yew in one of the interviews given by him had said that "The Muslim nuclear weapon – which already exists in Pakistan – will travel to other Muslim countries in the years to come". [6]

It would be recalled that the phrase 'Islamic bomb' was not coined by the Islamic fundamentalists, the Taliban or by Osama bin Laden. It was first coined in the 1970s and 1980s by the Pakistan establishment when they were seeking funding support for their programme from the Arab states. The connotation of an 'Islamic bomb' seems to have been lost upon US and Western think tanks who keep referring to the volatility of the South Asian theatre as a very likely place for a nuclear exchange. Their reasoning is not entirely correct. They have been missing the wood for the trees. Pakistan does not need an Islamic bomb to deal with India. A 'Pakistan' nuclear weapon would suffice. The connotation 'Islamic' has unmistakable supra- national and pan-Islamic overtones. It was meant to convey to the Islamic extremists the availability of these weapons of mass destruction for wreaking havoc against the enemies of Islam. These enemies are mainly in America and the West.

PART - II

What Comes After

PART - II

What Comes After

5

The Way Forward

Even before the US intervention in Afghanistan there were estimated to be well over three million Afghan refugees in Pakistan and Iran. A few million more Afghan refugees would be on the move in one direction or the other due to the war conditions obtaining and the unsettled conditions that could continue for a long time to come. Taliban and Pakistan training camps for *jehadis* may have been destroyed to a greater or lesser degree. In addition, many more may have been temporarily closed down on account of global pressure. However, there is no telling as to when the latent potential of the dormant trainees and their masters will again manifest itself and where. Therefore, unless massive global efforts are undertaken to provide modern education facilities for the children and unemployed youth in the refugee camps, wherever they happen to be, the problem of Islamic radicalism cannot be efficaciously dealt with. Of equal importance would be the need for health and family planning facilities. This latter aspect has not been given sufficient attention by the global aid agencies. The horrendous population increase in Afghanistan and Pakistan is one of the prime causes for the social unrest that is taking place. It attracts youth who are multiplying faster than the state's ability to create education and employment facilities.

The tragic happenings in Afghanistan would certainly lead to *post facto* recrimination, introspections and 'what might otherwise have been' type of speculations. There is no need to go back all the way to the partition of India to wonder as to how things could have shaped up if Pakistan had not started on the path of confrontation and concentrated instead on infrastructure development i.e., if instead of incurring such heavy outlays on military expenditure it had spent its scarce resources on human development to build a modern dynamic society. That was not to be. Speculation can, however, be attempted in revisiting the recent past. The recent past can be said to have commenced from the Soviet pull back from Afghanistan and the consequent collapse of USSR. In many ways Pakistan was in a comfortable position after its role in speeding up the Soviet departure. It was looked upon benignly by the Western powers led by the USA. China was well on the way to strengthening its relations with Pakistan. India, its long-term adversary was beset with difficulties; conditions in Kashmir had deteriorated sharply, its polity was in disarray and its economic situation precarious. Hence, looking around at the regional scenario the Pakistan government could have attempted, as first priority, to check the negative fallout from its involvement in Afghanistan by curbing the spread of small arms, rise in ethnic tensions and the growth of narcotics networks. The wiser course was not adopted. Pakistan went on a downward spiral and pulled Afghanistan along with it.

Ignoring the wrong turns taken in the 1980s and 1990s decades another fine opportunity for harmonisation with its neighbour India was missed when the military put a brake on the 'Lahore process' entered into by the political heads of India and Pakistan. Whatever the internal conflicts within the Pakistan establishment it can be safely surmised that had the Kargil misadventure not taken place and had Nawaz Sharif continued as the Prime Minister the outcome in Afghanistan might not have been the same.

In the years to come there will continue to be intense speculation in Pakistan, India and in many other parts of the world as to what the outcome in Afghanistan might have been if India and Pakistan had first sat down to work out a common strategy for the region after the September 11 tragedies in the USA. Had these countries acted in concert they could have obtained the backing of Russia and possibly China. USA and Europe would reluctantly have had to go along. With India in the reckoning the Arab nations would have supported the two subcontinental powers. It does not necessarily mean that the united Pakistan-India stand would have been against the American stand. It would have meant that the USA would have been obliged to take the subcontinental stand into consideration and possibly coordinate future policies with them as equal partners. Seeing that the Agra summit between the Indian Prime Minister and the Pakistan President was allowed to become the grounds for mutual recrimination, after the event, it seems highly unlikely that a joint Pakistan-India approach could have been worked out in the wake of the American ultimatum to various countries - of either siding with them or being construed (by the US) to be against them.

Be that as it may the Indo-Pak joint approach was an unlikely happening. What should not have been unlikely was the almost instantaneous capitulation by the Pakistan head of state to demands that would later become calamitous for Pakistan. Whatever might have been the nature of the ultimatum the manner of the abject surrender did not bode well for Pakistan or its head of state. National interest, in modern times, where dispensations change with increasing rapidity, becomes very subjective depending upon the caliber, character and stability of the wielder of power in a country, linked to the manner in which the person assumed the mantle.

Questions will be asked whether a legitimate head of state, duly elected, would have acted differently in the place of the military dictator. Did the precariousness of his own position dictate the national interest of Pakistan? Was the national interest, as defined by the incumbent, while succumbing to the American ultimatum, a collegiate decision before the fact of capitulation, or was it cobbled up *post facto*.

The self-appointed, self-anointed, President's conduct in the crucial period after the WTC bombings cannot be deemed to be an academic discussion since it led to a massive upheaval in the geopolitics of the region as a result of the US-led intervention in Afghanistan. Had the Pakistan President not lost his nerve at that crucial moment and insisted on a reasonable period of delay in communicating his decision *after* consulting with his colleagues and neighbours he could conceivably have altered the tenor of the dialogue that followed and the course of events as they unfolded. It is not inconceivable that an extensive dialogue with the armed forces and all segments of society, including the radical Islamist groups, would have led him to a different conclusion; to the effect that, regardless of all else, the US was in no position to take on Pakistan and Afghanistan simultaneously in the manner that it later acted in Afghanistan. In the latter case, China would not have given its consent and Pakistan might have emerged as an important independent arbiter of the future direction of the policy for Afghanistan. Time and again the destiny of nations appears to have been moulded by their leaders. Do leaders then encapsulate in their persona the fate of nations, or does destiny mock nations by throwing up leaders who will follow her dictates? Whatever the truth, the fact remains that destiny, while amenable to change, cannot be unmade. Nor can history be unwritten.

Had Pakistan harmonised its relations with India after the Shimla Agreement of 1971 where Zulfiqar Ali Bhutto obtained concessions of a type not available to a defeated nation the history of the subcontinent, Afghanistan and Central Asia might have turned out differently. That luckless country Afghanistan would not then have become the victim of Soviet aggression. It could have been induced to become part of a subcontinental confederation from Kabul to Colombo. The dominant players in Central Asia would, in that case, have been Pakistan and India, acting jointly to further the interests of South Asia as a whole. Pakistan chose to continue its confrontation with India. In the process it has certainly been able to diminish the role of India in Central Asia. The loss to itself and its western neighbour Afghanistan is of an order of magnitude higher than the loss inflicted upon India.

Indo-Pak Relations

The strategic overreach of the Pakistan military establishment linked to Islamic *jehad* has resulted in a strategic as well as existential nightmare for the people of Afghanistan and Pakistan; and to a greater or lesser extent to many neighbouring countries in the region. The physical suffering and demoralisation would be worse for the people of Pakistan who never had a say in what the military hierarchy was attempting behind their back; for most of the activities undertaken by the uniformed fraternity have never been freely debated in any real sense. The surprising thing is that after every debacle brought upon Pakistan by their military whenever they were in the ascendant, it has ended up by strengthening the military a few years down the line, once the ill effects of the debacle diminished to some extent after the restoration of quasi-independent civilian governments.

It is not easy to foretell at this early stage as to the long-term effects of the US intervention in Afghanistan, which, in actual fact, is a US military presence in the region, whatever its nature. The military government of Pakistan has allowed the basing of foreign troops on its soil for the express purpose of destroying the dispensations created by the Pakistan governments in Pakistan and Afghanistan from out of their own people. To put it bluntly, foreign troops have been 'allowed' in to quell indigenous unrest, the first time ever on the subcontinent after the retreat of colonialism from this part of the world.

It is an entirely different matter that under certain circumstances the right wing government in India might have offered facilities for US intervention forces. No matter how abhorrent the act, it would not have been on account of capitulation by the Government of India as has been the case with the military government of Pakistan. In the case of India it would, at worst, have amounted to sheer opportunism to add to the discomfiture of its adversary on its western border. In the reckoning of some people it would have been an act more shameful than the capitulation by the military head of the Pakistan government who, in reality, had not been given much of a choice by the Americans and whose economic situation did not allow too much room for manoeuvre. The people of Pakistan must now attempt to take the destiny of their country in their own hands. Outmoded, anti-modern, self-serving (for specific people or groups as opposed to the nation as a whole) theories of grandiose expansion plans into Central Asia or as defenders of pan-Islamism must now be given a decent burial. These have not only led nowhere, but have ended up in creating strategic nightmares for Pakistan from which there are no easy escape routes. Kashmir has been artificially played up for over 50 years to the detriment of India and the near destruction of Pakistan. Sacrificing the welfare and future well being of a nation for a hopeless cause to keep the military and mullahs in the ascendant in Pakistan is not a policy that can find favour with the silent majority of the people of Pakistan in the coming decades. Pakistan, if the country wishes to ever find a pride of place in the comity of nations, has to not only arrive at an accommodation with India, it has to determinedly undo much of the distortion in its policies that have led to the hopeless situation that obtains at present. The country has to reach out to India in the fields of cultural and economic exchanges. India and Pakistan have to jointly tackle the problems of poverty, population proliferation, lack of modern health and education facilities. A determined effort to jointly tackle the gargantuan problems facing them will bring prosperity to both countries and in a few short decades project the subcontinent as a major player on the global stage.

A people who are uncomfortable with their past can hardly be expected to feel comfortable about their future. There is a psychological disorientation that has been brought upon the people of Pakistan by their 'masters, not friends' when they imposed upon them dress codes, historical dissonances and the like, which were neither a true representation of their past nor a reflection of their emotional linkages with their subcontinental neighbours. The crisis that the country is facing gives them an unparalleled opportunity for allowing their 'suppressed histories' to reemerge. These are not required to either glorify or denigrate whatever emerges, but to look at it with a new wonderment that allows them to comfortably project into the future, based on the richness of their past multi-ethnicities. A *tabula rasa* approach could work wonders in reevaluating for themselves their future trajectory as a nation. Obviously the *tabula rasa* approach stops at Partition. It is neither in the interest of Pakistan nor India to revisit the bifurcation of the country. Any future revitalisation of their relationship must take off from the present and need not be a mere rectification of the pre-partition blunders of the past. Since the past fifty years have been dismal they should not be allowed to intrude into the future, which could turn out to be brighter than anyone might reasonably expect at this juncture.

However remote the possibility may appear at present, it would be worth examining, nevertheless, as a purely academic exercise, a route chart for reestablishing harmony between India and Pakistan in their quest for subcontinental equipoise. Some of the major steps that could be agreed upon might assume the following shape:

- An interim 25-year status quo in the state of Jammu & Kashmir with the LOC being accepted as a de facto boundary for this period.
- Permanent joint commission for addressing other outstanding disputes between the two countries in all fields other than Kashmir.
- Setting up a permanent Indo-Pak economic commission for speeding up of mutually beneficial economic trade agreements and Indo-Pak economic integration.
- Joint poverty alleviation programmes.
- Demilitarisation of the Himalayas as an Environmental Imperative.
- Joint tourism promotion packages.
- Cessation of hostility in global forums.
- Permanent joint commission for WTO negotiations.
- Free flow of media and publications between the countries.

- Cessation of propaganda and hostile comments against each other in government television and broadcasting channels.
- Exchange of students in technical and medical institutions.
- Exchange of military officers between the military institutions of the two countries.
- Removal of heavy artillery above a mutually agreed upon caliber and range of the weapons to minimum distance of 50 kilometers from the international border.
- CBMs for all forms of WMD.

Even before the September 11 events that shook the world and the consequent US intervention in Afghanistan, Pakistan's internal difficulties and economic situation had reached crisis proportions. Doubtless, it was in a position to add to India's discomfiture in Kashmir through the militant Islamic groups that it had sedulously nurtured. But any objective analysis would have shown that while India's economy appeared to be in the ascendant that of Pakistan had gone into a terminal decline. Its ability to create mischief in Kashmir remained unimpaired; its ability to wage war against India or retard India's progress had considerably diminished, notwithstanding the help received from China in the fields of nuclear and missile technology.

The events of September 11 changed the outlook for most countries in the world. For Pakistan the concept of strategic depth became overnight a quagmire from which it would find it difficult to extricate itself. It is not easy to forecast as to whether the turmoil in Afghanistan would be resolved in a few months or in a few years and whether it would be resolved in a manner with which Pakistan feels comfortable or whether it would add to Pakistan's insecurity. Conditions within Pakistan have become potentially so volatile that according to some experts Pakistan may take longer to come back to an even keel than Afghanistan. Simmering resentment between the remnants of the old order in Afghanistan and Pakistan may continue for decades. The seeds of mistrust that were sown by the *volte face* of the Pakistan military when they were confronted by the US could produce an abundant harvest of bitter legacy in the Pakistan provinces of NWFP and Baluchistan for a long time to come.

In addition to these existential problems the bitterness that would have crept into the elements of the Pakistan army emotionally attached to the Taliban could congeal into a permanent hatred of the upper echelons of the military hierarchy that was able to consolidate its hold only with US support. Hence it would not be wrong to say that the cohesiveness of the Pakistan military has been impaired. Impaired also to a very large extent would be Pakistan's ability to create problems for India in Kashmir or elsewhere. It is in the context of the existing reality in Pakistan that future relations with India should be looked at afresh, devoid of the misunderstanding and hatreds of the past. If anyone is in a position to attempt the resurgence of Pakistan as a dynamic member of the comity of nations it happens to be India. Should the agenda for a grand reconciliation (tabulated earlier) be examined in the light of joint progress in all spheres of Indo-Pak relations towards the strengthening of both countries it could provide a useful basis for moving forward.

Kashmir the *casus belli* for nearly three generations of Pakistanis has resulted in the decline of Pakistan. There can hardly be any two opinions on this count. It may, doubtless, have kept the military and radical Islamists in clover; Pakistan itself declined. Of late, on account of the inadequate control of the Pakistan state on the radical elements, a new thrust had been given to the Kashmir policy of Pakistan. Voices were being heard that the *jehad* would not end till it reached New Delhi: firebrand oratory or tendency to self-destruct? It could have been an admixture of both. Whatever the truth, the Pakistan government was unable or unwilling to keep a lid on the ferment. Currently the situation is quite clear as far as Kashmir is concerned. By the time the full effects of US intervention are felt, Pakistan's ability to interfere in Kashmir would have declined. Historians of the future might view this decline as a fortuitous happening for Pakistan. It would have freed Pakistan from the shackles of the past. It would represent the turning point in Indo-Pak relations. It could be said that a twenty-five year freeze, respecting the LOC as an international border, would work to India's advantage. That would be a correct perception in many respects. It does not automatically follow, however, that it would work to Pakistan's disadvantage in the long-term. Freed from the infirmity of Kashmir it would not have to worry about further emasculation at the hands of India in a future flare up that would have been well on the cards the way things were going prior to the US intervention. Pakistan could gainfully use the breathing space to reconstruct Pakistan where fragmentation has already resulted due to the intemperateness of past actions. The freezing of hostilities in Kashmir need not prevent the continuation of the dialogue to settle the question on a more permanent basis keeping in mind the interests of India, Pakistan and the people of the state of Jammu & Kashmir as a whole. Both sides should work out modalities for troops reduction and patterns of autonomy in their respective portions that allow for future harmonization according to the will of the people once the cross border tensions have simmered down. After the bitter harvest of the last fifty years all parties and especially the people of Kashmir who have suffered the most should remain alive to the need for keeping in mind the sensibilities of India and Pakistan in this regard. The inhabitants of the region should also undo the effects of their own mistakes of the past. A portion of the blame for the present state of affairs must also rest with them. Both India and Pakistan would have to set aside some funds to remedy the ecological devastation of the state that has resulted from over-militarisation and the military exchanges of the last five decades. One model for the `Demilitarisation of the Himalayas' put forward by the Eco Monitors Society at an international conference held at the India International Centre, New Delhi in November 1998 is reproduced at the end of the chapter (page 102) .

The other major suggestions for the long overdue harmonisation of the relationship between India and Pakistan should not be too difficult to progress. The permanent joint commissions, not subject to the ups and downs of political interactions between the two governments, should have permanent staff and secretariat. They could meet alternatively in New Delhi and Islamabad at laid down periodicity. They should be manned by experts from the two countries as well as non-resident Indians, Pakistanis and other experts who could further the cause of jointmanship between the two countries. The joint commissions, or the two governments, could themselves hire a reputed international consultancy for undertaking a study for the joint economic development of South Asia. The terms of reference could include, inter alia, joint production, joint bidding for contracts in third countries, merger of shipping lines and airlines and host of allied aspects that could project South Asia as the major player in the world markets of the coming decades. Agreements between the two countries in regard to trade relations already arrived at in principle should be speedily implemented in a time bound manner.

Once the initial confidence building measures in the military field have come into effect parallel joint studies could be undertaken for the next stage of military rapprochement. Areas of interest in the second phase, say between 2006 and 2010, could include: partial troop reduction, exchange of instructors at designated military establishments, joint Indo-Pak brigades for UN peace keeping operations, joint production of defence items in selected sectors, consortium approach for investment in military high tech areas and other fields where commonalities can be developed to the benefit of both nations. Obviously, this would be a gradual process linked to a sincere removal of the potential causes for future misunderstandings. At some point in time the process would culminate in a treaty of perpetual amity.

It is axiomatic that the type of rapprochement envisaged cannot take place without a complete cessation of hostilities and hostile propaganda. Not only should the two countries desist from denigrating each other in international forums or in their government sponsored media, they should be seem to be actually supporting each other in world forums. Since decisions in perceptions are bound to develop in many areas in the years ahead, as is generally the case even between neighbours who have not been fighting each other, a thought can be given to the setting up of a Indo-Pak dispute settlement tribunal for resolving the contentious issues that may come up in the future. To be credible, the tribunal comprising 11 members would consist of eminent jurists whose names should be approved by the Supreme Courts or the governments of both countries. There would be 5 members each from India and Pakistan. The 11th member who would preside over the tribunal would be an eminent international jurist, from any country in the world, whose international reputation for jurisprudence, wisdom, integrity and impartiality had been globally established. Before the setting up of the tribunal both countries would pass legislation in their respective parliaments to abide by the decision of the tribunal in all cases referred to it. Separate clauses can be inserted in the 'joint tribunal act' to be enacted in the two countries for cases that can be referred to the tribunal and those which can only be settled through negotiations between the governments or the International Court of Justice at The Hague.

Poverty alleviation, health care, population stabilisation and education are areas in which both governments would have to make heavy outlays should they truly wish to improve the lot of the people. Without addressing these areas at the highest priority and with the utmost dedication and professionalism no real progress will be possible for either India or Pakistan for the coming years. Illiterate, unemployed and burgeoning populations have been a drag on both countries since they achieved independence. If conscientiously examined, it will be found that many of the ills affecting the two countries are directly attributable to lack of progress in redressing these ills.

It should be the ordinary citizens of Pakistan themselves, who are not part of the theological struggle to capture political power in order to impose medieval Islamic codes on the hapless people, to fight against the mesmerisation and programming of a million young people into vessels of intense hatred. Hatred like love flows outward from the source in concentric circles. The greatest effect (the most severe effect) is felt at the source and in the circles nearest the source. A few years down the line the contamination of the innermost circle will be complete, unless the Pakistan citizens fight back to cleanse their land of hatred and bigotry.

It is possible that the present, cataclysmic events will help dissipate the dross that was seeking to cover the sublime face of Islam. The obscurantist, dogmatic, intolerant and violent face of Islam being shown to the world today is not its true face.

Demilitarisation of the Himalayas as Environmental Imperative

(Presentation made on behalf of Eco Monitors Society at the Eco Revival Summit 98 on 9th November 1998 at the India International Centre, New Delhi)

The military dimension has generally prevailed over most of the other dimensions of human existence since the dawn of history; but never to the extent that it has in our century. Coming even closer to our day and age it now tends to submerge most other dimensions; to the detriment of the planet as a whole. As a landmass the Himalayas, and the regions adjacent to the great mountain chain, have the dubious distinction of playing host to perhaps the largest concentration of military forces and destructive weapons systems anywhere in the world. The collective concentration of the forces of China, India, Pakistan and few other states could soon destroy one of the most magnificent natural habitats of the world. Individually, some countries like India and, possibly Nepal, Bhutan and China "have" started perceiving at the edges of their military vision that all is not well with the ecology of the region. In non-military segments awareness has come that an irreversible decline may already have set in. All the countries that derive sustenance from the mighty Himalayan sources have subconsciously realised that the day of reckoning is not far off. The audience present here does not have to be reminded of the suffering caused to hundreds of millions of people by unprecedented floods. In this presentation we will look at the inter-regional dimension of the problem in order to highlight the fact that unless the countries of the region come to their senses and join hands to reverse the eco-destruction of the Himalayas the future generations of Chinese, Indians, Tibetans, Nepalese and Pakistanis will not have much left to fight over. The eco-restoration of the Himalayas is now an ineluctable survival imperative for over a billion people living in and around the Himalayan region.

The eco-revival plan being put forward for consideration divides the larger portion of the Himalayan region into five segments: i.e. areas west of the 75° E meridian, that is the Pakistan-Afghanistan sector; the India - Pakistan sector, the India-China sector and other relatively dormant sectors. The first sector west of the 75° meridian is outside the purview of today's presentation being the battleground for the power play of too many outside powers. We will take the remaining sectors turn by turn.

Indo-Pak Sector (Jammu & Kashmir Sector)

The J&K sector can again be divided into two sub-sectors i.e. Ladakh sector and areas to its north and remainder J&K.

In the Ladakh sector the major dispute centres around Siachen. The highest battleground in the world has created, in addition to the human suffering undergone by troops of both sides, environmental devastation whose effects will only be known once the troops pull out. Tens of thousands of tons of human waste, oil and lubricants and other contaminants have penetrated the snowy vastness, not to mention the millions of rounds of small arms ammunition and mortar and artillery shells. We grew up with the phrase "pure as the driven snow". It has acquired a different meaning in much of the Himalayan landscape. We recommend an immediate de-militarisation of the Siachen region along the following lines:

Non-military joint commissions to verify the exact position of the belligerents on the ground. After verification the documents to be deposited by the respective governments at the International Court of Justice at The Hague. Both countries would give written undertakings not to change the status quo after troop pull-back for a minimum period of twenty-five years. In case of infringements, the ICJ to be empowered to impose heavy fines on the defaulting party. Concomitantly, China would give a written guarantee not to, in any way, take advantage of the demilitarisation to the detriment of the countries pulling back their troops. Other nations are not required to get into the act.

- After submission of the documents to the ICJ complete demilitarisation up to designated lines would be effected within 180 days.
- The prime ministers of India and Pakistan to jointly dedicate a memorial to the dedication and fighting spirit of some of the best soldiers in the world fighting under conditions which could be termed as the utmost in human endurance.

Thereafter, joint Indo-Pak scientific teams to study the environmental impact of the Siachen folly and remedial measures for limiting damage to future generations.

India-China Sectors

The India-China sectors can again be further subdivided into three zones from the point of view of past hostility as follows:

- **No skirmish zone** (since after the occupation of Tibet by Chinese troops)
- **Zones of continuous tranquility** (for over thirty-five years i.e. since after the 1962 conflict)

- **Zones of hostility** (or skirmish zones)

  Having delineated the sub sectors we recommend the following pattern for gradual demilitarisation of the Sino-Indian border and ecologically fragile zones of Tibet.

- In the first instance the Siachen demilitarisation model to be applied to the first two zones of the Sino-Indian border i.e. the no skirmish zone and the continuously tranquil zones. Similar deposition of documents before the ICJ along with identical pledges and penalties for infringement. China being a permanent member of the Security Council with veto powers that body has been given a wide berth.

- Establishment of joint eco restoration commissions to undertake joint eco restoration work without prejudice to either country's stand on the boundary dispute.

- Pledge before the ICJ that neither country would ever use the eco restoration zones for military activities in the future or to launch any military operations through those areas.

- The Chinese government to set up an independent commission for phased de-nuclearisation and demilitarisation of Tibet in anticipation of international movement of the nuclear powers in that direction. Regardless of the rate of that progress the Chinese government to unilaterally chalk out a massive twenty-five year programme for the eco-restoration of Tibet. World Bank and the Tibetan diaspora to assist.

- The Government of India in concert with the Royal Nepalese government to chalk out similar twenty-five year scheme for the full scale eco-restoration of the Himalayas in the entire sub-Himalayan and trans-Himalayan regions. Ex servicemen Gorkha pensioners and Indian ex-servicemen to be fully incorporated in this mammoth task.

At this juncture we have outlined a bare-bones scheme for the eco-restoration of the Himalayas on behalf of the Eco Monitors Society. We have already done considerable work to flesh out the scheme. At this conference, however, we would like to invite the views of the participants to refine the scheme during the sessions devoted exclusively to the eco-restoration of the Himalayas.

6

The New Uncertainties

Many of the certainties that were a given in the USA since long were demolished in one fell swoop on September 11, 2001. The events of that day and the days and weeks that followed have brought in new uncertainties, not only for USA but many countries around the globe. Countries that are antipodes away from both USA and Afghanistan. If there can be such a thing as prime players or prime actors in this affair they can be said to be Pakistan, USA, Saudi Arabia and Afghanistan. The order in which these countries have been mentioned is also relevant. It was USA that created the Mujahideen and bin Laden. USA, however, was the catalyst. The base material on which, or through which, the change was sought to be wrought was Pakistan. To begin with Pakistan had a clear choice. Had it not offered itself as the frontline state to become the proxy for the Americans in their war against the Soviets in Afghanistan there is nothing very much that the US could have done about it. Not only did the military head of Pakistan at that time, General Zia-ul-Haq not demur, he actively sought the role for Pakistan and threw himself into it with a faithfulness that went beyond the wildest expectations of USA. It is a moot question whether a democratically elected dispensation would have jumped in the same manner.

The other major benefactor of Pakistan during this episode, and which remained a benefactor till well after the Soviets and Americans had left the scene, was Saudi Arabia. Here again, Saudi Arabia offered Pakistan large sums of money to carry out, or to continue with their joint programme, for the radicalisation of Islam, not only in the subcontinent, but in many other parts of Asia as well, especially the newly emerged Central Asian Republics. Pakistan offered itself as the vehicle for `fundamentalising' Islam as a prelude to the denigration of Islam in a manner that has not taken place since the inception of Islam. Speculation will remain for a long time to come as to whether the role played by Pakistan was truly in the cause of Islam – as interpreted by the military and the mullahs – or whether it was debased in this manner to further the geopolitical ambitions of the Pakistan military and their supporters in the Muslim clergy.

When looked at in this light, it will be seen that except for Afghanistan, which was the victim and remains the victim, the other countries, Pakistan, USA and Saudi Arabia were playing games in the unfortunate country, with no regard whatsoever to the fate that could befall Afghanistan due to their machinations. Afghanistan is bleeding horribly. Pakistan started to bleed a bit later. America and Saudi Arabia, in their different ways, have started to bleed now. Afghanistan's agony is terrible. The extent of haemorrhaging that Pakistan, USA and Saudi Arabia will have to undergo will depend on their post-September 11 strategies and philosophy. When there is such turmoil in the neighbourhood, India and the subcontinent automatically get affected. Central Asia and the rest of Asia, including Eurasia, also get affected. In the analysis that follows greater emphasis will be placed upon the new uncertainties that are likely to shape the destinies of Pakistan and Afghanistan, followed by the other countries who come into the ripple effect.

Pakistan

It has been mentioned elsewhere in the book that no durable structural adjustment in Afghanistan would be possible without Pakistan itself undergoing structural readjustment in the first place. Obviously, the most immediate effect relates to: the economy, the stability of the current military hierarchy and the internal struggle to redefine Islam. The last aspect, i.e., the need to redefine Islam has to be looked at first because on its outcome will depend the direction that can be taken by the Pakistan government and, in a relative sense, its economy. Percentages giving out the numbers backing radical Islam have been variously estimated from a low of 10 per cent to a high of 35 per cent after September 11, 2001. Should stability return to Afghanistan and be followed by a modicum of stability in Pakistan, then it is quite likely that the elements supporting radical Islam may dwindle down to a figure nearer the lower figure of about 10 per cent. A discussion on this aspect that has now become fundamental to the reconstruction of Pakistan as a responsible member of the comity of nations becomes essential. Should it come about that more than one-third of the people of Pakistan hold views on a basic issue at such variance with the views held by the remainder population, Pakistan may find it extremely difficult to come out of the *cul de sac* of religion into which it has fallen. A major split of this nature will also affect governance and create a permanent divide between the polity, the military, the educated liberal class and, what is worse, within the polity and within the military. Governance will, in that case, remain at low ebb for a long time to come.

When analysing the governance patterns that could evolve hereafter in Pakistan it is to be noted that the churning within Pakistan could, in a manner of speaking, become as formidable as the churning in Afghanistan, in some respects. Doubtless, the army in Pakistan will remain the strongest element in the foreseeable future. It would be wrong to infer therefrom that the army remains on the pedestal that it occupied after the military coup of 1999. The respect for the army has dwindled considerably. There are several reasons for this decline. Firstly, deep down there is a feeling among the people of Pakistan that having had control over the affairs of Pakistan for so long the army has again betrayed the nation by losing control over the situation in Afghanistan to the extent that, backed by some elements within, its progeny went and attacked USA with an intensity that was bound to provoke massive retaliation. It did not require more than ordinary commonsense to anticipate – for those in the know – that any US retaliation against the Taliban would automatically have a devastating effect on Pakistan. Therefore, the military and the ISI did not safeguard the interest of Pakistan. Juxtaposed to it is the fact that when confronted with the American ultimatum the head of the Pakistan military lost his nerve. There is really nothing that the US government could have done had the president of Pakistan demanded a few days for consultation before acquiescing to American demands. It would have allowed time for strategic consultation with China, several other staunch backers of Pakistan, and a far wider and deeper examination of options available to Pakistan. As things stand, the consultations that took place were mostly *post facto*, after certain communication lines carefully nurtured over decades with some of the closet allies, had become permanently impaired due to the indecent haste with which the decision was taken. Regardless of what the future holds in store for Pakistan, the Chinese and the supporters of Taliban in both Pakistan and Afghanistan are hardly likely to forget the grand betrayal. Viewed dispassionately, the Pakistan head of state - having become one through a process of self-anointment - buckled under American pressure sooner than anyone would have expected, even the Americans. That many other nations rallied behind the US on account of the enormity of the terrorist act is a separate issue because their support did not affect them directly. In the case of Pakistan, no thought was given to the effect of the capitulation on the Taliban, China and others. It was an odd action, without parallel in recent times.

As a result of the hurried capitulation by the Pakistan head of state other consequences that would follow over a period of time were built into the act of acquiescence. These were the transfers in the army hierarchy and the ISI carried out under *external* pressure, again in haste. They could add to the stresses in the army, which was already reeling under the burden of capitulation to American demands and the consequent betrayal of its closest ally, the Taliban and, by extension, Osama bin Laden. A factor that has to be taken into consideration would be the simmering resentment that would be building up in the officer cadre of the Pakistan army due to the gradual diminishment in the stature of the Punjabi dominated elite that has been replaced by non-Punjabi generals in such large numbers and at such speed. Whether this results in counter coups or not, the fact remains that the cohesion of the Pakistan army has been effectively sundered in just a few short weeks.

When decisions are taken in haste, or forced upon recalcitrant supporters under external pressure, they release forces whose outcome becomes indeterminate. To cite an example, a decision was taken to replace the Pakistan army corps commanders in NWFP and Baluchistan by non-Punjabi generals whose ethnicity coincided with the ethnicity of the people in those provinces. It may have been a bold move, or it may have been a decision enforced by the US masters, or it may have been a desperate gamble. Whatever the case may be it is a type of decision that professional armies do not normally take. At the very least it can set dangerous precedents. It could lead to wholly unanticipated outcomes.

While looking back at Pakistan's predicament in the fateful days following the September 11 attacks, after the top echelons of the US government recovered their wits, a thought has to be given as to what, in fact, constitutes the 'national interest'. The term is simple enough with a straightforward connotation. In recent times its overuse, misuse and abuse has put a big question mark on its earlier interpretation. The Pakistan head of state cited national interest for his quick capitulation. Future historians in Pakistan will debate for a long time whether the decision was taken in the interests of Pakistan or to preserve the hegemony of the Pakistan president and the Pakistan army. It was said that besides Kashmir a major factor in the decision to capitulate was the security of Pakistan's nuclear capability. Before going any further into this argument the possible outcomes of non-acquiescence have to be taken into account. The first thought that comes to mind by hindsight is that non-capitulation could have actually strengthened Pakistan's position in more ways than one seeing the near impossibility at that point in time of the US being able to progress military operations without taking Pakistan on board. Therefore, it is possible that the national interest cited by the Pakistan president was a smoke screen. It is very much on the cards that the incumbent was unnerved by the proof that was shown to him of his close associates' involvement with Osama bin Laden and *Al Qaeda* - so much for national interest. As public morality declines further it will become increasingly difficult to distinguish between supreme national interest and supreme self-interest. Not only in Pakistan, but in many other countries of the world as well.

It could not be lost upon the people of Pakistan that the policies pursued by their governments resulted in physical US military presence in Pakistan and direct intervention in Afghanistan. Seeing the magnitude of the threat posed due to the type of terrorism being indulged in by the *Al Qaeda* networks and their supporters most governments, including those opposed to US hegemony, welcomed or supported the US intervention. They realised that, US unilateralism notwithstanding, only that country had the resources and the international support to undertake the task of eradicating this scale of terrorism in the world. For the present the threat has manifested itself mostly in the US and the West. At a later stage, it could as easily have targeted many other countries, especially the Muslim countries whose present governments were being opposed by the radical Muslim groups. Be that as it may, the fact remains that the US government will hereafter continue to dictate terms to the military government of Pakistan and its successor governments, ushered in at the behest of USA, for a long time to come. On the positive side it could lead to a lessening of the threat of civil war and fragmentation of Pakistan.

Should Pakistan use the generous aid being offered to Pakistan as a client state of the USA in its fight against radical Islam intelligently, it would represent an ideal opportunity for the country to modernize its education and health services. Women who represent 50 per cent of a nation's human capital could also be gradually brought into the mainstream. Under this scenario Pakistan's economy could stabilise and productivity restored. Pipelines from Iran as well as Central Asia would transit through Pakistan on to the subcontinent and beyond bringing prosperity for the provinces of Pakistan not only on account of the transit fees, but also an account of the billions of dollars that would have to be spent in the construction of the pipelines, mostly in Pakistan. It would provide employment to large sections of the population and give a boost to Pakistan's economy for a long time to come. With increased prosperity there would be a corresponding decline in fundamentalism. It would lead to further economic cooperation with India. At that point the Kashmir question would have become largely irrelevant.

The rosier outcome described above is only one of the possible outcomes. Since the creation of the Taliban has raised the stakes for Pakistan the defeat of the Taliban due to the relentless American offensive could end up by decimating or scattering the Taliban dispensation in Afghanistan as presently constituted. They may simply fade away or go underground to embed themselves into the adjoining provinces of Pakistan and in the *madrasas* whence they came; to surface again at an opportune moment in a different garb. One of the critical aspects to emerge from the September 11 crisis has been the realisation that the eradication of terrorist cells - in many parts of the world - deals only with the business end of the phenomenon of radical Islam. It does not address the heart of the problem - the mass production of indoctrinated young fanatics in an assembly line process, constituted by the thousands of *madrasas* spread in Pakistan and adjoining areas. Therefore, until the *madrasas* are either closed down or brought under state control, with their curriculum approved by the state – and here state implies a dispensation that is desirous of change – there is little scope for effectively dealing with the terror that could continue to be unleashed by radical Islamists in the years ahead. It needs to be reiterated that women's emancipation, population stabilization, modernization and humanising of the education curriculum, linked to improved health infrastructure across the country, is perhaps the only way to remove the threat of future *talibanisation* of the country and reactivation of global terror networks, the successors to *Al Qaeda* and bin Laden.

Pakistan is not likely to see an early return to democracy; on account of the strengthening of the military regime that would be taking place due to American involvement in the affairs of Pakistan and the continued support for the Pakistan military, and in the military, the pro-US leaders. The reason being that the USA simply cannot afford to upstick from Afghanistan and Pakistan till it is convinced that the September 11 type of tragedy can never be visited again on the USA or its allies. Presently the Pakistan–Afghanistan region is the only region that has the wherewithal to clandestinely keep the USA on the run or in a state of semi- permanent anxiety. The threat emanates from this source; and until the day that the source has been sanitized with the same care, precision and perseverance as any deadly virus that escapes from the laboratory the US can never rest in peace. Eradication with such thoroughness cannot be undertaken without slaving the Pakistan military and its intelligence offshoots to the US quest that, incidentally, benefits Pakistan and most of the world – both Islamic and non-Islamic. There would be rewards for the Pakistan military, and Pakistan, as has been discussed earlier. In the fast changing world of today no society can afford to be static. The currents and counter currents flowing through the region have jolted Pakistan society as never before. At the present time the people of the country are afraid to go against USA due to the recent happenings. Pakistan society is worried about the future of Pakistan and the breakdown of societal cohesion that has taken place and is still taking place. They are alive to the collateral damage caused to Pakistan through the human displacements that are being forced on Afghanistan. They are frightened by this seething mass of humanity that has undergone such horrendous suffering for more than a generation. If its frustration goes any deeper it will seek vengeance. The most likely target for the pent up emotion and suffering by the human jetsam and flotsam represented by the refugee camps would be Pakistan. The Soviet intervention is now an old story. The more recent sufferings can be laid directly at the door of Pakistan and the geopolitical ambitions of its military rulers. Regardless of the US largesse that could follow a political settlement in Afghanistan a military dispensation can never face the challenge posed due to the latent hatred buried in the bosoms of the population, both new and old, residing in NWFP, Baluchistan and a few other places. Therefore, it is in the interest of Pakistan and the region that the political process in Pakistan is gradually restored. The military will be loath to give up political power. Here again, they will have to be coaxed by their benefactor, the USA. Unrest in Pakistan can be anticipated and controlled by the announcement of an irreversible process for the restoration of democracy under US guarantees, in a phased programme lasting three to five years. The stages of the restoration would be clearly spelled out and strictly adhered to.

It would hardly be an exaggeration to state that the Pakistan generals have ended up by making their region a war zone. Forces from many parts of the world will gather here to decide amongst themselves the future of Afghanistan and quite possibly Pakistan. The generals have become pawns in a game which they started but did not know how to end. It ended by blowing up in their face. The land of the Pure has allowed people from the land of the impure to come and establish military bases in their country. When and if the foreigners leave, nobody knows; certainly not the people of Pakistan or the Pakistan generals. All decisions will be taken in Washington and not Islamabad. Not even in New Delhi. The generals still do not talk of a return to democracy. They want to use Afghanistan's - and Pakistan's - misfortune to strengthen their hold.

Their policies could lead to clashes within Pakistan. While they may not represent a 'clash of civilisations', they could certainly end up in a clash of similar dimensions between the Pushtuns of Pakistan, who number approximately 20 million out of Pakistan's 140 million population, and the Pakistan military. Nobody knows against whom the theologically fanaticised products of the ten thousand odd *madrasas* will turn. The Afghanistan refugees in Pakistan have suffered the most. No matter how it all started their present suffering can certainly be laid at the door of the military leaders of Pakistan. They too represent a combustible mix. Their misery is being exploited by local contractors. It is difficult to foresee as to who will be able to control this resentful, seething mass of humanity once it decides to break out from the confines of the refugee camps in their millions. Will they too have to be bombed out? This time by the Pakistan military forces!

Ghettoisation of Pakistan

The people of Pakistan would have learned to their consternation that they cannot have it both ways. Their country cannot be deemed to be the progenitors of the most virulent form of global terrorism – they can change the wording, but it will not change the reality – and yet hope to move about freely in the world. Nobody is going to stop their generals from moving about because they are used to switching loyalties and are now co-opted by the USA in its fight against the very same terrorism that they were abetting a short while ago. The result of a poll reported in a London newspaper some time back showed that if given a chance, 62 per cent of the people polled wanted to leave Pakistan for greener pastures. The paper went on to say that a similar poll conducted in the early 1980s when General Zia-ul- Haq took over put this figure at a low of 18 per cent [7]. Irrespective of its accuracy, it shows a disturbing trend. In spite of the loud noises of a pure Islamic state, carved out of India, not many Pakistanis seemed to have a permanent stake in the country of the pure. Whatever their past predilections they will have to learn to stay put for a long time to come unless they choose the route of illegal migration. The fact is that hereafter hardly any country in the world is going to allow Pakistanis to come and settle in their country. People of Pakistan origin who had entered illegally will now be hunted down and deported. It may take an entire generation for normalcy to return. The citizens of Pakistan have only themselves to blame. They may have been able to trouble India by raising the bogey of Islamic *jehad*; they have clearly overplayed their hand. Since ghettoisation creates its own psychosis and insecurities the moderate elements in Pakistan must now take their affairs in their own hands and push out the military and the mullahs, who have brought their country to this pass, and fight for a return to democracy and a liberal Islamic dispensation. Once they embark on this route steadfastly and purposefully, they will find great support from many quarters. In the course of time the rest of the world will also start welcoming them back as responsible members of the global human fraternity. The people of Pakistan have to ensure that all fresh aid given to them is channeled into modernizing their education and health systems. They have to give a thought to stabilising their population and allowing their women to play their part in bringing Pakistan on to the global arena as respected equals.

Afghanistan

Before undertaking its military action in Afghanistan the US government was worried on account of being sucked into the quagmire of Afghanistan in the manner of the Soviet Union not so long ago. The comparison held good up to a point. The Soviet intervention had been opposed by most of the countries in the world. Secondly, the reverses faced by the Soviet Union were largely due to the bases provided by Pakistan and the not inconsiderable financial and military support given by Saudi Arabia and the US respectively. In the present case the US intervention was supported by practically the whole world against a regime detested by most countries in the world, outside its circle of support in Pakistan. Not very much military or financial support was likely to reach the Taliban from any source other than the clandestine support that would continue to be available to it by elements in the Pakistan army, the ISI and the collections organised by infuriated Muslims opposed to US bombings. Moral support and manpower support would be likely from adjoining provinces in Pakistan.

The problems for the Americans in Afghanistan could result more from the latent potential of the Taliban to re-emerge in Pakistan, or elsewhere on the subcontinent, at a later date with a view to regaining its foothold in Afghanistan. As part of the US strategy many local commanders supporting the Taliban are being induced to change sides or to distance themselves from the Taliban. This strategy may work in the short run. It could create problems at a later date. Tribal leaders who are buyable could just as easily be repurchased by others, the price being right. Hence, to base post-intervention governance strategy for Afghanistan on the shifting sands of purchased loyalty might not turn out to be a sound proposition. The US has no choice but to go all the way to remove the influence of the Taliban in Afghanistan as well as their spawning grounds in Pakistan. The Pushtuns being the largest ethnic grouping in Pakistan will no doubt have to have a major representation in any future Afghanistan government. Before that they will have to be permanently separated from the Taliban.

A stronger UN presence in the post-military intervention phase represents the best option for stability in Afghanistan in the coming years. King Zahir Shah's return could become a workable option - as an interim measure only - towards a more permanent settlement. The outline strategy for a UN backed reconstruction of Afghanistan is tabulated below:

Post-Conflict Strategies for Afghanistan

(in case of successful intervention)

- *Stationing of UN forces for deployment in selected areas only.
- US back up forces. (In bases outside Afghanistan).
- **UN administration.
- ***Disarming in areas liberated.
- ****Re-framing the Afghan constitution.
- 'Loya Jirga'.
- Return of former king, Zahir Shah. (Should it remain a viable proposition).
- Repatriation from Afghan diaspora.
- Restructuring liberated Afghan Areas.
- Restarting judiciary, civil services, setting up a minimum operational infrastructure.
- Re-forming Afghan police force.
- Stationing of standby international force for guaranteeing sanctity.
- International guarantees against aggression from Pakistan, and other neighbours.
- Neutral state – UN recognition.
- Merger with Northern Alliance forces under terms supervised by the UN.

- Education Package.
- Rehabilitation Package.

*The composition of the UN force should be multilateral; as has been the case for UN forces of this nature in the past. The question of ethnicity and narrow interpretations on the basis of religion should not be allowed to come into UN functioning. It would set a bad precedent that could lead to complications for the future of all support operations. The concept becomes abhorrent to the UN ethos.

**It would be an interim administration in selected areas only with built in scheme for transfer of administrative functions to the Afghan people in phases depending on the degree of stability achieved. Transfer of functions, rather than power, would be the norm for the initial phases. For example, the restructuring of education, women's emancipation and revitalisation of the health sector could be handed over to competent and qualified Afghan professionals before moving on to other sectors. It would have to be ensured that the process of transfer of power does not lead to factionalism and future discord. The aim of the UN administration has to be to provide a viable model for restoration of peace in war torn regions. It would be wrong to assume that an impartial administration that was seen to be working for the revival of Afghanistan would not be appreciated by the majority of the people who have undergone untold suffering for much too long. Tribal loyalties are strong. However, the fact remains that nearly a third of the population in refugee camps outside Afghanistan is now a heterogeneous mix. This population constitutes the largest segment of the Afghan population. Their displacement, loss of privacy and extreme deprivation would have changed their perception, character and outlook on life. At the very least it would not be the same as before. The process of refugee rehabilitation itself would have to follow a programme and pattern very different from the rehabilitation process that was carried out earlier. Future rehabilitation programmes would be required, *inter alia*, to take into account the following: de-mining; safe areas for setting up tented or prefab camps. The refugees may have to be re-located with adjacent schooling and health facilities as an interim arrangement, while the people help in clearance schemes for re-cultivating and re-building. Land rights, redistribution patterns in areas where entire villages or families have been wiped out would require to be gone into. Referenda may have to be held from camp to camp for post-relocation strategies in designated areas after ascertaining, and respecting to the extent possible the wishes, as to whether the returnees wish to be governed by common civil codes - or laws applicable in most democracies - or by old tribal customs. Resettled communes could be co-opted to decide the development patterns for the areas in which they are being resettled; at a later stage the meshing in would be coordinated up to the provincial level; finally tie up would be done with the national grid. Taxation patterns would have to be worked out in consultation with the people; the same would apply for ecological rehabilitation; water purification, electrification and restoration of irrigation channel schemes. The UN would help develop local packaging and marketing units for local produce.

***The returning refugees would be encouraged to form local militias with police functions for their resettlement in designated areas till the national police grid is established. The type of arms that can be carried would be specified. No heavy weapons would be allowed to be retained by returning refugees. Phased removal of heavy weapons would be undertaken sector by sector once a national gendarmerie is established. Meanwhile, the multilateral force would ensure that law and order is maintained. At a later stage sealing of borders would have to be undertaken for preventing the inflow of fresh war materiel.

****It would be an important exercise that could be undertaken simultaneously, regardless of all else, by inducting selected persons from the refugee camps, amongst others, to work out a model constitution for Afghanistan in the 21st century based on the national ethos and aspirations, but keeping in mind the global reality of the new century. The committee so constituted would be assisted by constitutional experts co-opted from countries that are practicing democracies. It would function under UN aegis. Once the draft constitution has been prepared it would be put before the 'loya jirga' for comments. It would be separately approved, with modifications considered necessary, by elected representatives who would be a deemed constituent assembly. Thus far the exercise would have been carried out under UN supervision. The constitution so adopted would have the provision for a constitution review after ten years by a fresh constituent assembly should a two-third majority of the elected representatives at that time desire that such review take place.

There will be many pitfalls, missteps, meandering before arriving at the selected goal. However, clarifying the intent at the very outset will help to rally most of the Afghan people round to it and pre-empt undesirable activities and initiatives on the part of Afghanistan's neighbours. Stability in Afghanistan will automatically lead to greater stability in Pakistan, Iran and the Central Asian Republics. Peace and tranquility will start flowing outwards from one of the most troubled areas of the world.

On the initiative of the US, a Special Security Council resolution to this effect should be considered.

Concomitantly, a referendum can be taken of the people in the refugee camps in countries neighbouring Afghanistan. It can be made, to the extent possible, a participative process. The dispossessed Afghan refugees today make up one of the largest segments of the Afghan people. The referendum would be conducted under UN supervision.

By the looks of it Afghanistan's agony is unlikely to be over in a hurry. Its past misfortunes can be laid at the door of Pakistan, more than anybody else. The fixation on strategic depth never for a moment took into account the interest of the Afghan people or the misery that would result from Pakistan's interference. Therefore, for any condition of peace to obtain in Afghanistan requires a hands-off policy by the Pakistan military establishment; a very unlikely proposition unless a *restraint* is imposed on it through UN Security Council mandated sanctions in case of infringement.

The Northern Alliance has been artificially bolstered by the support of Russia, Iran and India acting in concert for their own reasons. Its position has been further strengthened through US intervention. All the parties involved are again serving their own interests. Hence, a neutral Afghanistan based on a UN led restructuring on the Swiss pattern seems to be the best bet for the country's long-term stability.

In case the varying factions, or their backers, fail to arrive at accommodations that serve the interest of Afghanistan as a whole, a partitioning of Afghanistan and Pakistan may take place along ethnic lines. The contours of this partitioning could be along the following lines:

> Consolidation of the Northern Alliance to the North of the Hindukush.

- Designated areas in Central and Western Afghanistan with separate status.
- Remainder Pushtun dominated area of Afghanistan as an autonomous entity.
- Kabul to be a joint capital with a Central authority functioning under the UN with separate sectors of the city allocated for the 3 entities created in Afghanistan. The status of the city of Kabul would be somewhat similar to the status of Chandigarh in India. It is centrally administered and serves as the capital of both Haryana and Punjab. In Kabul the UN administration would be removed after 25 years or earlier should the three entities agree upon the reunification of Afghanistan in a peaceful manner under international guarantees. The perimeter of Kabul could be extended considerably to include Bagran and other adjoining areas. Up to five million refugees could be re-settled into a Greater Kabul principality. Comprising over a quarter of Afghanistan's post-intervention population, it could choose to remain a separate entity and play a major role in the future governance pattern for Afghanistan. After reconstruction Kabul could emerge as the principal city of Central Asia, a veritable cross-road between Central and South Asia. Its Vatican like status would be internationally guaranteed. It could become the first UN Peace City of the 21st century.

A possibility that cannot be discounted is the creation of a greater Pushtun state with Pushtun dominated areas in Afghanistan incorporating portions of NWFP across the Durand Line. It would result in a slight truncation of Pakistan, but then that is the price that Pakistan might have to pay for its interference in Afghanistan's affairs and the suffering caused to the Afghan people due to that interference.

The refugee crisis in Afghanistan has worsened considerably in the recent past. It could become much worse in the months ahead depending upon how soon a modicum of stability is restored in that country. Estimates of the numbers of refugees in Pakistan, Iran and the CAR vary. At the very least the number could have exceeded 3.5 million. It is not inconceivable that in worst-case scenarios the figure may go up, should the conflict become prolonged. The world seems to have adapted to the misery of the Afghan refugees. In future the actual amount of money required to barely keep body and soul together for the refugees may prove hopelessly insufficient. Disease and infant mortality could take a devastating toll. These are known outcomes. It has happened before in refugee camps all over the world. Therefore, while the fighting rages inside Afghanistan the UN relief agencies, the Red Cross and aid donors, mainly Japan and the West, should devise newer strategies for making the refugees self-reliant and to prevent young girls from being forced into prostitution.

That Pakistani contractors are exploiting the refugees is well known. Pitiable wages are being paid to young children working up to 16 hours a day. It has come out that local contractors pay 15 Pakistani rupees for spinning one kilogram of wool. Similar starvation wages are paid for other backbreaking chores. It should be possible for the Western nations or UN agencies to create income-generating works in market related trade offs. For example, Western consortia, working through the UN relief agencies, could provide initial funding for labour intensive employment works and contract to take back the produce at globally competitive rates that provide a reasonable return on their investment. The UN agencies, in turn, would deduct a laid down percentage from each person's wage for setting up schooling and health facilities for the children in the refugee camps. Schemes of this nature will not only reduce casualties from disease and hunger, but would help to restore the self-respect of the migrants who would then be creating the facilities from their own labour; and not simply as dregs subsisting on global charity. A percentage of the boys and girls, schooled on modern education curricula, could be sent abroad for training so that they come back as experts to revitalise their country's economy.

Albion At It Once Again

What was generally suspected is being confirmed by scholars sifting through post-World War II records; that the US policy in many parts of Asia, especially the subcontinent, was influenced in the early years to a large extent by British mandarins and intelligence services. These policies may have served Anglo-US interests in the second half of the 20th century. It ended up by pushing US policy into certain grooves from which it never really emerged till the end of the Cold War. Throughout that period British interference - and behind the scenes diplomacy - generally tended to undermine India's interests. Coming to the present crisis it can be shown that British policies also contributed to the spread of radical Islam. It would not be an over statement to say that British governments can, to some extent, be held responsible for the spread of Islamic radicalism in the Western world. It is fairly well known that some of the earliest Islamic centers came up in the UK. These had started functioning by the 1970s. The money for the centers was provided by Saudi Arabia and the clerics from Pakistan. Together they started training adherents for the spread of a more illiberal brand of Islam. On several occasions concern was voiced by their European counterparts to the British government about the destabilising activities being carried out by the Islamic centers in UK. The pleas of their continental allies, even during the worst years of terrorist activity in Europe in the 1970s and 1980s, fell on deaf years. It is only now, after terror having been inflicted upon their closest ally USA, that the British government is taking steps to curb the activities of radical Islamic elements in UK. As to how effectively the measures announced for curbing terrorism are actually implemented only time will tell.

Britain has once again become an important partner of the USA in shaping US policies in Pakistan and Afghanistan. Its 'humint' resources in the region may still be superior to those of USA. Its centuries long occupation allows it special insights. The insights come accompanied with the prejudices and bigotries of the post-colonial era of the 20th century. British actions in Afghanistan and Central Asia in their capacity as the strongest allies of USA need to be watched by all the countries in the region, including the people of Pakistan.

Central Asia

Neither the world nor the states of Central Asia themselves realised at the time that the centuries old Russian expansion would unravel at such speed, almost overnight, so to say. The surprising aspect is that these states were hardly wanting to opt out. Most were reluctant to do so. In their decade long independence after the break up of the Soviet Union they have faced many ills. These include: internal bickering amongst them, ethnic tensions, maldistribution of resources, scramble for influence and their hydrocarbon reserves by outside powers, externally sponsored Islamic revivalism and, of late, terrorism supported by the Taliban regime in Afghanistan. The fact that almost all the republics are old style dictatorships has bred corruption and inefficient administration. Of the many ills that plagued them the most worrisome appeared to be terrorism sponsored by the Taliban. The problem was exacerbated by narco-trafficking through their territories.

Before the September 11 events the Central Asian states had tried to set up joint mechanisms with Russian prodding for facing the threat posed by the radical Islamic groups whose prized goal was the Ferghana Valley. Russia had given considerable support for jointly dealing with the common threat. It had maintained a division-sized force on Tajikistan border with Afghanistan. The threat of Islamic radicalism had also resulted in a common front with China. After settling their boundary delineations with China, the states having a common border with that country joined Russia and China to form the Shanghai group whose members decided to coordinate their policies to face common threats. The group was renamed the Shanghai Cooperation Organisation.

The short recapitulation relating to the Central Asian states and the regional efforts to jointly face emerging threats to the region indicates the general direction in which efforts were afoot for preparing themselves for an eventual Pakistan supported Taliban breakout into Central Asia for bringing in the Taliban brand of Islam to the region. Their hopes for continued reprieve hung literally by a thread in the form of the resistance put up by the Northern Alliance. Although the area held by the Northern Alliance prior to the suicide attack elimination of General Ahmed Shah Masood, the Lion of Panjshir represented just about 5 per cent of the area of Afghanistan not under Taliban control it prevented, nevertheless, the Taliban from directly ingressing into Central Asia.

There is a major difference between the fighting potential of the Northern Alliance and the Taliban or any other force that comes up subsequently in the Pushtun dominated regions of Afghanistan. The Northern Alliance is not a natural grouping. It lacks long-term cohesion and stability. At least one or two of its present commanders would be amenable to switching sides, as was the case in the past. The Northern Alliance could, in all probability, remain deficient in manpower, economic and military resources. Hence, unless common strategies are worked out between Russia, Iran and the CAR to hold the line of the Hindukush, a much more natural defence line, come what may, there is little prospect for the safety of the CAR or the potential threats that could emerge to Iran and some of the Russian republics. Russia and CAR could use this period to first eliminate the internal threats posed by radical Islamist groups within these countries before embarking on expanding their reach in Afghanistan. Concomitantly, the larger umbrella organisation with a central planning staff, headquarters and logistics base, jointly sponsored by Iran and Russia would also have to be formalised in a more professional manner to enable the reining in of maverick generals prone to private initiatives with opposition forces. The US could maintain a permanent liaison mission. India could be co-opted into the joint planning process *ab initio*.

All these countries should realise that irrespective of the present situation and the post-intervention outcome in Afghanistan in the near term, the successors to the Taliban, which could even be a chameleon like variant, would have enough manpower resources and backing from Pakistan - or elements in Pakistan - to reemerge as a strong force for radical Islam in a much more virulent form unless complete eradication during the present intervention is effected. A US presence could provide a modicum of long-term stability in the region provided that the US does not start pursuing strategies that undermine the interests of the other countries forming the coalition, notably, Russia,

Iran

Thirty years ago Iran surprised America and the Western world with the Khomeini revolution that overthrew the Shah of Iran. At that time as well the Americans were taken by surprise at the rapidity of the collapse of the military regime nurtured and supported by them since the overthrow of Mossadeq. What is even more surprising is that the Americans had a large military presence in Iran in the form of advisers. At the beginning of the 1970s Richard Helms who had been active in the plot to overthrow Mossadeq had returned to Iran as the US ambassador, after heading the CIA. The Americans had infiltrated the SAVAK and all segments of the Shah's government. Extensive training with the Iranian armed forces was a regular feature. American advisers were present in many formation headquarters. Iranian armed forces had been largely equipped by USA, UK and a few other Western countries. The number of Persian speaking agents of the US in practically every Iranian city was large. Yet the revolution, when it came, caught the US napping. What was lacking was not sufficient intelligence inputs, but a mindset in the establishment in stateside USA that failed to assess the mood in the *bazaar* in Tehran, Isfahan and elsewhere. To anyone sufficiently fluent in Persian the differences in outlook of the officer cadre – largely American trained – and the rank and file would have become apparent. How did the Americans with such formidable and intrusive presence fail to detect the underlying unrest?

A study of the Iranian revolution of 1979 is highly educative. It brings out clearly the pattern of perceptual deficiencies that can arise in the establishments of countries that have preconceived ideas and fail to have independent bodies that have the stature to force the governments to take into account formulations that may be diametrically opposed to establishment views. The US does not lack for respected institutions that retain their independence. They get submerged, however, by others whose conformist nature tends to drown out as a collectivity - due to sheer mass - the contrary views as being mere aberrations. In Iran in the 1970s the Americans were convinced that with the formidable array of weapons available to the Shah of Iran the armed forces could meet any challenge to the stability of the regime. Tragically for the Americans the regime was brought down not from superior or matching weaponry but by the strength of an ideology and an unarmed populace that could not have been quelled by the latest variety of airplanes and tanks. In many ways September 11, 2001 is a repeat of what happened in Iran in 1979 with the advent of Rohullah Khomeini.

The old adage that one seldom learns from one's mistakes, and is condemned to repeat them came true for the USA in a mere 30 years or so. The signs were all there. These could have been picked up (tentatively) in Afghanistan and in abundance in Pakistan. Enough activity had been set in motion in USA itself. Considerable light has been thrown on the intelligence lapses *post facto* after the tragic events of the WTC and Pentagon attacks. What is not sufficiently realised by people outside the charmed establishment circles is the fact that in their obsession to set up the National Missile Defence (NMD) system, quite a bit of the uneasiness that would have obtained among many intelligence experts was artificially suppressed so as not to deflect attention from the massive outlays being made to the NMD sector at the cost of outlays that should have rightly gone to counter the asymmetric series of emerging threats. Even a cursory examination of the NMD debates worldwide when the so-called rogue states threat was being pushed to the skies along with the star wars would show that experts had constantly been highlighting the increased probability of low level threats in continental USA.

The point of departure for the digression in the previous paragraph was the threat posed to the Western world by the Islamic revolution in Iran and the unease felt around the world by its proclivity for pan-Islamism. These activities suffered diminishment due to the intense suffering that the Iranians had to undergo during the Iran–Iraq war of the 1980s. It bled Iran as it did its adversary. Iran has come out of the worst traumas of the revolution phase and the war with Iraq. It has emerged, contrary to earlier US thinking, as one of the more stable and responsible states in a region that has built in instability. The new dispensation in Iran represents a voice of moderation and sanity. At the present stage Russia, China, India and the European countries would consider Iran to be the natural pivot for regional stability in Central Asia as well as the Middle East. Should the USA come around to this point of view – and it seemed to be veering towards it – the country can become the center for an enlightened, accommodative and liberal Islamic resurgence of the 21st century. The CAR would be comfortable with this development. Many of the Middle East countries could gradually gravitate towards this thinking. Turkey could welcome it. In Afghanistan itself, the Northern Alliance can be brought within the fold. Initially Pakistan, and elements in Afghanistan instigated by that country, would be opposed to the spread of Iranian influence as a moderating force in the region. However, with the economic prosperity and stability that could result, the benefits would automatically flow to the rest of Afghanistan and subsequently on to Pakistan. The process could take anything from two to twenty years. It is a direction that appears promising.

Iran's policy vis-à-vis Afghanistan has to be assessed multi-spectrally. Before the US intervention, Iran's Afghan policy was a function of its regional strategy for Central Asia, and as a part of its attempt to overcome the isolation and encirclement being imposed on it by the US. Iran is in need of long-term stability and regional allies that it can depend upon. Viewed from Tehran its military situation could become worrisome. Iraq, whatever its present state of enfeeblement, is a permanent threat. After the rise of Islamic fundamentalism in Pakistan both Afghanistan and Pakistan could remain a threat to Iranian interests in the region. The US military presence in the Gulf and more recently in Uzbekistan and Pakistan, not to mention the formidable naval deployment in the Arabian Sea, can only keep Iran on tenterhooks. As it looks ahead Iran would perceive both Russia and India as stable partners, if not allies. China too could fall into the same category, but at one remove. Suspicions of its closeness to the Pakistan military regime and the Taliban could never really be discounted. Russian influence as well as the strategic nature of Iran's alliance with Russia is likely to grow on account of Russian military supplies and the nuclear plant being built by Russia.

Iran has had its share of Afghan refugees. Its concern with the developments in Afghanistan was heightened by the rapid progress of the Taliban towards the north; for capturing the remainder portion of Afghanistan, in the hands of the Northern Alliance, and the Taliban's attempts to eliminate the non-Pushtun minorities through wholesale killings in the areas captured by them. As it anxiously watched the spread of the Pakistan–Saudi Arabian initiatives in Central Asia it felt impelled to provide assistance to Shii groups in Afghanistan and Pakistan. While all this was going on it resolutely moved ahead in another field – it refined its oil linkages with Central Asia. Here again it found a useful ally in Russia. The Iranians were always suspicious of the Taliban. Before the recent anti-climax there was a phase when the Taliban were being supported both by Pakistan (overtly) and the US (tacitly in support of their oil interests) for their push northward into Central Asia. Even China had arrived at an understanding with the Taliban and was reportedly extending aid to them. For these reasons Russia and India were again perceived to be the only countries in the region whose interests would coincide with Iran for a long time to come; in the domains of geo-strategy as well as geo-economics. In the case of India there remains a long history of cultural affinity.

Middle East

The Middle East mosaic of Islamic nations has several facets. It would be best to take a look at some of the important players in the region as their support and tacit backing for what was essentially an Anglo-American intervention in Afghanistan would be important for the post-intervention strategies. Although not directly involved in Afghanistan, except for Saudi Arabia, due to the lack of geographical contiguity, the silent support of the Middle East nations was important to the US in its global efforts to neutralize the terrorist threat posed to it and to many other countries in the world. Looking first at Saudi Arabia, its position, in some respects, could become nearly as uncomfortable as that of Pakistan. There are two main reasons for it. The first reason relates to the solid financial support that it has been providing since long to the spread of conservative Islamic dispensations. In several countries in its neighbourhood it was tantamount to direct interference in their affairs although the moneys were generally channeled through Pakistan and its intelligence agencies. As to how much of this money was retained in Pakistan and recycled by that country for its own ends will remain an unanswered question. Whatever its initial intentions in funding this movement in other countries it must share a portion of the blame for radicalizing Islam to make it an instrument of terror. That nobody directly accused the Saudis for their indirect interference can be attributed to the enormous clout of the Saudi royal family, due to its oil wealth and guardianship of Islam's holiest sites.

Although the governments, including India, that suffered due to the Pakistan–Saudi nexus in spreading radical Islam chose to remain silent, one of their own nationals, Osama bin Laden had no such qualms. The latter's dispute and subsequent flight from his home country has been too well documented to bear repetition. Suffice to say that irrespective of what transpired in the past Osama bin Laden, dead or alive, now represents a far more potent threat to the survival of the Saudi governing hierarchy than any threat posed to them prior to Osama's projection on to the world stage as the defender of Islam. The magnitude of the threat, linked to the seething unrest among ordinary Saudi citizens, is such that the Saudi royal family is in a bind. They are alive to the resentment building up to the US presence in Saudi Arabia; and yet they are unable to expel the Americans who remain the guarantors of their continued domination. Like the Pakistan head of state, they too have become hostage to each other's survival imperatives. These three countries, USA, Saudi Arabia, Pakistan - unnatural allies in another unholy embrace - had come together the first time to project Pakistan as a frontline state against the Soviet occupation in Afghanistan. Only twenty years have elapsed between the first and second collaborations. The difference being that while America comes in as a country, the governing elements in Pakistan and Saudi Arabia are no longer sure of support of their own people. They are both hostage to the continued American presence in the region.

Coming to Iraq, the country has remained in the forefront of the fight against American dominance since its defeat at the hands of the US led coalition in the Gulf War under the senior President Bush. Whatever their thinking at the time the US won the war, but in many ways it lost the battle for Iraq. It did not carry the war to its logical conclusion. In the twenty years since his defeat Saddam Hussein's stature has increased manifold in the Arab world as a symbol of rock-like defiance of the Americans. The more the Americans devastated his country through sanctions and bombings the more the world began to sympathise with Iraq. The stage has now come where USA and Britain must go it alone. The US must seriously consider bringing Iraq back into the fold by means other than its existing policy towards that country. It cannot, for various reasons, arrive at any reasonable settlement with Saddam Hussein directly. Axiomatically, USA cannot be seen to be capitulating to Saddam Hussein by stopping the bombing and allowing for the lifting of UN sanctions without adequate safeguards. The US has been the global hegemon after the Cold War. Psychologically, the US establishment may find it difficult to ease up on that role, especially in the case of Iraq. Statesmanship and the need for isolating the current perpetrators of global terror demand that the USA hand over the role of bringing Iraq back into the fold, with full safeguards relating to WMD, by co-opting the European Union and Russia as intermediaries. Unless the latter are allowed a free hand the initiative could become a non-starter. Should there be a positive outcome, it alone could result in greater stability in the region. Saddam Hussein would have to eschew any further interference in the Gulf States or in the Israel-Palestine stand off.

Turkey

Turkey has an important role to play in the uncertain period ahead; primarily on account of many unique features that distinguish modern Turkey from the rest of the Muslim world. To begin with Turkey, as opposed to some other great empires of recent times that collapsed after the First and Second World Wars, is reasonably comfortable in its post-Ataturk identity. In its dealings with the rest of the world Turkey does not let nostalgia for the great Ottoman empire of the earlier centuries intrude. They are proud of their Muslim heritage, but would unhesitatingly join the European Union in a secular mould rather than any Islamic union. Their armed forces are professional and secular in outlook. It has offered to provide troops for any post-US intervention tasks in Afghanistan.

At the present juncture Turkey becomes important to the world on several counts, the most important of these being its being there as a role model. Many Muslim generals in the past have considered themselves as following in the footsteps of Kemal Ataturk. They failed. Beside themselves nobody else saw them in the Kemalian role. The main reason was that their driving ambition was limited to holding on to power and not for the modernization of their countries through a wrenching break from medievalism. They neither had the stature nor the military prowess for their assumed rules. The only battle that they had won was generally a bloodless coup against the civilian governments in their country. Notwithstanding the drawbacks of modern day Ataturks in Islamic countries the example of Turkey remains important for ushering in modified Turkish patterns in arriving at a more durable and stable governance model for almost the entire Muslim world from the Mediterranean to the Indian Ocean and up to the Caspian and Black Seas. There is hardly any predominantly Muslim country, which can be referred to as a stable democracy. Most Muslim nations are dictatorships, ruled by traditional tribal chiefs who became kings in the post-colonial era; or dictatorships formed by military strongmen. In the case of the CAR, they are ruled by satraps from the Soviet era.

The prospect of democracy in the Muslim world seems as remote today as it was fifty years ago. Unless concerted efforts are made for bringing in real democracy, in stages, there is unlikely to be any let up in the seething discontent, which simmers below the surface. Much of this discontent is actually against their own dictatorial dispensations that deny freedoms available to modern societies around the world. Since the people in these countries are unable to express their resentment against their own rulers it becomes easy to mobilise them against external enemies of Islam, perceived or real, on whom many of the intractable internal problems can be projected. America, the great Satan, can be made to fit the bill admirably for wrongs, real or imagined. USA fits all sizes for the latent, cooped up hatreds in the Muslim world.

Whenever the dictatorships in the Muslim world are overthrown they are unlikely to be replaced by democratic processes. They are likely to be overthrown by radical Islamist forces unless these are kept in check; or by another strongman promising reform, but settling down into the same groove. Therefore, intellectuals and the modern educated classes in Muslim societies must now themselves start thinking seriously of ways for bringing democracy and freedom in their societies. Just as there is pan-Islamic radicalism the time may have come for a pan-Islamic liberal wave to free their societies from evil customs that deny freedom to all their citizens. Western countries supporting the US intervention in Afghanistan must interact with the Muslim societies with a view to helping their transition to harmonious relationships with the rest of the world. The Turkish model, for at least some of the countries, represents a reasonable halfway house to full democracy.

Egypt

The Egypt of President Hosni Mobarak of today is no longer the Egypt of the heady days of Nasser's pan-Arabism. What could have been a great rallying movement for the Arab world collapsed on itself and Nasser's shattered dreams at the hands of the crushing defeat inflicted by Israel in 1967. Nasser died shortly thereafter taking along with him the dream of a unified Arab world from Tripoli to Oman. Egypt retained the shell of a United Arab Republic. In stature it was diminished considerably. Many lessons from the events leading up to 1967 can be drawn by hindsight. One of the most tantalizing questions remains as to what would have happened if the UN Secretary General, U Thant had not acceded readily to Nasser's request to pull out United Nations Emergency Force (UNEF) troops.

Perhaps the most important lesson for the forces that have intervened in Afghanistan after the September 11 events is that an enemy decisively defeated is the most desirable outcome; if it leads to a lasting solution when total war is declared against a country, like the call given to decisively cripple USA in every way possible. In spite of the lessons of past interventions, many faulty, the USA has no choice but to eradicate fully the dispensation in Afghanistan that gave rise to the terrorist networks that have played havoc with USA and its overseas interests. If these are left half defeated, or temporarily paralyzed, they will show their hand again; in a far more decisive manner, at a time and place of their choosing, to hit back at the USA. There can be no ad hoc solutions to problems that have festered over a period of time. There can be no negotiations with terrorist organizations built around radical Islam. America has already created an icon around the persona of Saddam Hussein, after leaving the work in Iraq only half finished. Either the USA should have negotiated with Saddam Hussein after his defeat to reintegrate Iraq in the global mainstream if possible, or it should have continued fight till Saddam Hussein had been replaced by a more moderate government in Iraq, acceptable to the forces that intervened during the Gulf War.

Egypt under Hosni Mobarak is relatively stable, propped up considerably by US support, both military and financial. It is an essential pillar for the continued viability and existence of Israel in its present form. In that respect both Turkey and Hosni Mobarak play an important role in maintaining the status quo in that part of the world. It is, however, a fragile stability as it is centered around Hosni Mobarak's ability to keep Islamic fundamentalism in Egypt in check. Were Hosni Mobarak to be overthrown and replaced by a government formed around militant Islamic groups, Israel's days could be numbered, regardless of whether it possesses nuclear weapons or not. Fundamentalist Islamists would attempt, thereafter, to break out from the bridgeheads already formed in southern Europe. Europe would be unable to withstand the demographic surge from the other side of the Mediterranean. Therefore, Europe has as much at stake in the post-US intervention strategies in Afghanistan as the USA.

Saudi Arabia

Saudi Arabia has been considered the linchpin for US interests in the Gulf. What was an important relationship before Iraq's invasion of Kuwait became the cornerstone of American geo-strategic interests in this region. Since it was the biggest producer of oil its importance to the US, Japan and the Western Alliance was critical. In many ways Saudi policies relating to oil flows have determined OPEC policies and to a large extent global macro-economics. Saudi Arabia - and taking a cue from it the Gulf States - helped to revive the US economy, which was in a decline at the end of the Cold War, after the war was over. They not only underwrote much of the cost of the deployment for the Gulf War, they collectively projected the US economy into its upward spiral during the 1990s by purchasing military equipment running into tens of billions of dollars. They threw a lifeline to the military-industrial complex of the West. It was resuscitated. Additionally, by investing their oil wealth in the West they have benefited the economies of those nations. In the process these countries – Saudi Arabia and the Gulf States – went into an economic decline compared to the economic resilience that they had shown after the oil price rise of the 1970s.

Nobody seriously doubts that the Kingships and Emirates in the region are maintained to a large extent through their Western trained and Western equipped armed forces. After the Gulf War these have been buttressed by the Anglo-US military deployments in and around the Persian Gulf. US Central Command which was a relative late comer on the scene could soon become the most central of all US Commands, literally so.

During the Cold War years it was the Shah of Iran who was reckoned to be the closest ally of the US in the Middle East. During that time the Iranian military purchases from the West were so large that the stability of the Shah of Iran was of paramount importance to the military-industrial complex. To keep their production lines going was for them as important as maintaining geopolitical stability, possibly more so. Some distancing started taking place when the Shah showed signs of independence after his military capability had started assuming astounding proportions, creating an imbalance in the region. The decline when it came was sudden and swift. It surprised the Americans and the Shah in equal measure. Even the elite Imperial Guard caved in almost overnight.

Saudi Arabia has assumed a pivotal role analogous to that of Iran of the 1960s and 70s. Overthrow of the Iranian monarchy by the return of Ayatholla Khomeini turned the Western geo-strategic checker-board on its head. The ripples of the Khomeini revolution were felt well beyond the shores of Iran and its neighbourhood. The question that should be uppermost in the minds of the US and the Western Alliance as also for Iran, Russia, India and the region as a whole should be: 'What will be the effect of the overthrow of the Saudi monarchy by an escaped bin Laden landing up in a sealed capsule - in the manner of Lenin - in Saudi Arabia to assume the leadership of the Saudi people'? In the present case, bin Laden does not have to manifest himself physically like Lenin or Khomeini. Any of his chosen successors could have the same effect. Would an eventuality of this nature have a domino effect on the Gulf States? Ironically, the Western Alliance may come a full circle. Saddam Hussein of (secular) Iraq could turn out to be the only real bulwark against an Osama type take-over of the Arabian Peninsula. It is not improbable that bin Laden has been training Arab volunteers for such a take-over in Saudi Arabia, the Persian Gulf and the Middle East; wherever an opening is found in the coming years for the establishment of a bridgehead. The tangled skein of the Saudi Arabian royal family has thrown up contradictions from time to time. The clan is no longer as cohesive as it once was. The stakes have become enormous for the USA. Should an adverse situation develop in Saudi Arabia, followed by the Gulf States, it could not only play havoc with the world economy, it could end up by actually dethroning not so much the Saudi royal family, but the USA from its perch as the reigning superpower of the world. Osama bin Laden declared war on the USA well before September 11, 2001. He may yet prove himself to be wilier than the US. Ultimately, with its gigantic military and economic assets, which include the assets of the entire industrialised world, USA may win the war against Osama bin Laden. It would, however, have been a close run thing.

Whether by design or as a result of the fall out of September 11 events the possibility that Osama bin Laden, or the movement he represents, was planning a take-over in Saudi Arabia via the US actions cannot be ruled out. Ascending to power in Saudi Arabia would meet all of bin Laden's goals for the short, medium and long-terms. As the ruler of Saudi Arabia he, or his successors, would be able to turn out the US occupation forces from the Arabian Peninsula. His control of the Saudi oil wealth and the hold it would give him over global oil prices would automatically allow him to dictate terms to the USA and its allies. He would hardly waste time in terminating the lucrative defence contracts with the USA and those countries of the Western world that remained hostile towards him. Indications are already surfacing that the House of Saud is divided. Divided also is the support that the Saudi clerics have been extending routinely to the Saudi rulers. Oil, the very commodity that boosted the global influence of Saudi Arabia, is selling below the OPEC range of $22-$28 per barrel. Due to the economic recession the oil prices could remain below the $20 per barrel level for a long time to come. Such drops while being of concern to the Saudi government could be a matter of rejoicing for bin Laden or his successors. Saudi

Arabia, the most important member of the OPEC cartel and the principle exporter of oil, relies heavily on its oil revenues for the welfare programmes of Saudi citizens, almost literally from 'womb to tomb'. A price of $22 per barrel allows the Saudi government to maintain its welfare schemes, defence outlays and the royal family expenditures at the comfort level that maintains the expenditure – revenue equilibrium. Prolonged depreciation in the market would add to the woes of the Saudi government. For Osama bin Laden or his successors it could turn out to be a cause for rejoicing.

Jordan, Syria, Israel, Lebanon

The Palestinian issue is no nearer solution now than it was in 1948. Israel started its fight with its back to the wall – with its back to the sea literally – and it continues the fight in a state of siege – both physical and mental. For a moment the Oslo agreements offered a ray of hope. Israel seemed to be on the verge of an agreement both sides could have lived with. It was hardly a formulation for lasting peace, but it would have lessened tensions all around and allowed for the first time in the troubled history of the region a reasonable hope for a less frightening future. The opportunity was allowed to slip away. Perhaps, never to return. Not on the same terms.

On the face of it the issue relates to the Palestinian question. At the deeper level it involves Lebanon, Syria (and the Golan Heights under Israel's occupation), Jordan and its large Palestinian population, and the Sinai Peninsula of Egypt. Of these Arab entities Jordan has been co-opted into the Western fold through continued support for the Jordanian royal family and military and financial backing. Jordan's temperateness allows Israel breathing space, as did its peace agreement with Anwar Sadaat of Egypt. Through various ups and downs relations with Jordan and Egypt have remained on an even plane. It is not the intent in this book to go into the intricacies of the Palestinian question. The issue has been raised to address a fundamental question, which will have a bearing on global stability in the 21st century. The question is: 'What right do the Muslims in Pakistan and Afghanistan have to kill innocent civilians in the USA because they are upset with Israeli actions in the West Bank and Gaza strip'? The question is very basic. Muslims in Pakistan and Afghanistan have enough existential problems of their own to be thinking of interfering in affairs of another state with whom they have neither any geographical contiguity and which does not even form a part of their neighbourhood. Unless this logic is challenged and demolished there can be no peace between religions or between nations in the 21st century, and even beyond.

Extending the argument further, 'should India send its forces or train terrorists to go and fight for the Indian community in Fiji because they are being troubled or killed by the Fijians'. Or in Bangladesh where the minority Hindu population is being ravaged? Again, 'should countries in Europe train terrorists to go and fight the Muslims in the Moluccas and Celebes because Muslim fundamentalists are killing Christians in the hundreds in these Islands'? There is no end to the doctrinal perversity that justification of this nature throws up. It is human nature to sympathise with the underdog or with people of the same faith, kinship or ethnicity - be it linguistic, territorial or religious. Going deeper into the basis of such reasoning can one extend the logic to other fraternities? Should aficionados of jazz go and terrorise people in Japan who may be persecuting members of jazz clubs in some towns in that country. The fundamental mistake made by the UN, and the Western world has been to allow the perversity of the logic used by Islamic fundamentalists to stand. It should have been rejected on the very first occasion that it raised its ugly head. It is a quagmire into which the whole world can sink. The Palestine question needs to be settled for stability to come into the Middle East. It is an important issue that does not brook delay. It should, however, be de-linked from religious ethnicity and Islamic fundamentalism.

Russia

Russia gave its endorsement to President George W. Bush's strategy for fighting global terrorism, without delay. Once US intervention commenced in Afghanistan and the outlines of the post-intervention strategies of the US and its allies started taking shape President Putin might have felt some anxiety. Whatever the standpoint, a long-term convergence of interests in the region – as opposed to fighting global terrorism per se - between USA and Russia would seem unlikely. No doubt Russia had to pull back considerably from Central Asia after the collapse of the Soviet Union. In the Yeltsin years its economy had gone into a tailspin and the unrest in Russia itself hardly allowed any room for manoeuver beyond Russia's borders. However, after a measure of stability had been attained under President Putin, Russia could not have for long ignored its interests in its immediate neighbourhood in Central Asia.

Being mindful of its reduced influence in world affairs and the precarious state of its economy Russia felt obliged to arrive at strategic accommodation with China. Therefore, while both these countries are quite alive to the problems posed by Islamic terrorism in their own countries they would not welcome a permanent US military presence in Central Asia or even Pakistan, for that matter.

Russia agreed to intelligence sharing and coordination of military strategies. Looking into the future Russia's plans for the Northern Alliance may not remain for long in total conformity with those of the USA. Certain commonalities would, nonetheless, remain. For both countries the Northern Alliance represents more than a trip-wire against resurgent Islamic fundamentalism spilling over into Central Asia, in the case of a revitalized post-Taliban force emerging again from the seminaries in Pakistan. Hence, both countries would realize that for the long-term the threat of Islamic fundamentalism emerges more from Pakistan than Afghanistan. The cohesion of the Northern Alliance is superficial. Its fissures could be deepened by an American backed Uzbekistan playing a lone hand through their protégé. The seeds of future discord have already been sown. Russia would be more inclined to coordinate its strategies with Iran. It becomes vital for both these countries to keep a firm grip on the situation in Northern Afghanistan. As the Americans consolidate in Uzbekistan Moscow's wariness will increase. Uzbekistan, in return for support would expect financial help from USA as also help to fight the Islamic militants who have posed a big threat to the present regime.

Time and again history has demonstrated its penchant for scuttling the games men play when they get too ambitious and start disturbing the harmony of their existence by coveting other people's territory. Only two decades ago Pakistan was in the frontline of the struggle to push out the Soviet Union from Afghanistan. The combined efforts of Pakistan, USA and Saudi Arabia were successful. Not only did the Soviet forces quit Afghanistan, but shortly thereafter the breakup of the Soviet Union resulted in Russia being pushed out of Central Asia as well. Pakistan through its policies became the instrument just ten years later for the return of the Russians to Central Asia. Exquisite irony. Had the CAR not been worried about the Taliban threat to their countries they would not have welcomed the Russian presence back into their countries so soon after the breakup of USSR. Russia is not only back; it is back with a vengeance. What Russia does in the years ahead will once again be a cause of concern to Pakistan. The civil war in Afghanistan has strengthened Russian influence in Central Asia. There was a time, after the demise of the Soviet Union, when the CAR felt that trade route through Afghanistan could perhaps be their lifeline to the outside world. Had this come about Afghanistan, Pakistan and India would have linked up with Central Asia in a way that would have benefited the entire region. These hopes were belied. The turmoil in Afghanistan increased their geographic isolation and pushed them back into the Russian security and economic basket. Hereafter, Russia will have to ensure that it creates strategic depth for itself by not only ensuring the strength of the boundary with Afghanistan along the Amu Darya; it would, in fact, endeavour to see that it retains a direct or indirect military presence all the way up to the Hindukush. Till, at least, the time that a neutral Afghanistan emerges under full international guarantees for its neutrality. Under the circumstances the US would be unable to deny Russia this degree of comfort; until the time that Pakistan and Afghanistan are de-Talibanised down to the *madrasa* level. This could take anything between five to fifteen years. The US would have scarce choice, but to go along with the Russian strategy.

USA: Carpet-Baggers to Carpet Bombers

The present turmoil in Afghanistan can be largely attributed to the US' inability to grasp the political reality in the region after the Soviet withdrawal; and Pakistan's action and its consequences, of overtly supporting the fundamentalist groups in Afghanistan. Saudi Arabia and Pakistan were USA's closest allies when fighting the Soviets in Afghanistan. The USA had a policy for getting in. It did not have a policy for getting out. It simply walked away. For a superpower that won the Cold War and dreamed of global hegemony, it was an inexplicable lapse. The US government is worried that the Stinger missiles that were allowed to fall into the hands of the Mujahideen might be used to knock out US military aircraft and helicopters supporting the ground forces in Afghanistan. Their real worry should be that these missiles do not turn up in the USA, to wreak greater havoc in that country.

The US had been aware all along that following the end of the war against the Soviets, Pakistan and Saudi Arabia continued to provide funds for Afghanistan war veterans for the recruitment and training of Muslim volunteers from other Islamic countries in various terrorist training camps that had been opened in several areas of Pakistan and Afghanistan. These inputs were ignored because Afghanistan had ceased to be a priority foreign policy objective for the US after the Soviet withdrawal at the end of the Cold War. Whatever residual interest was maintained was not for keeping a watch on the newly emerging threat. It was for containing Iran and for supporting US oil companies for exploiting the hydrocarbon reserves from the CAR. Clarity of vision and purpose were both sacrificed to commercial interests. In this very volatile region geo-economics prevailed in an isolated manner over geo-strategy. America is paying the price.

Another area of concern to the US was the flow of narcotics from the Islamic crescent. The US had hoped that the Taliban would crack down on drug trafficking. To their dismay UN reports confirmed that there was an increase in opium output. The Taliban extended control over 80 per cent of the narcotics trade in the Golden Crescent. Additionally, US intelligence agencies had long suspected that contrary to the Taliban pledge to root out terrorism and drive out international terrorists, the Taliban ended up by providing sanctuaries to hundreds of Arab 'Afghans' who were reportedly on the FBI list as suspects for attacking US establishments. Even at that stage the US under-estimated the threat posed to their global interests from the elements being trained in Pakistan and Afghanistan, specifically for that purpose.

The US remains in an unenviable position in Afghanistan. Its military problems are compounded by an overwhelming image problem. While David and Goliath comparisons would naturally come to mind a Labour Party member in the UK is said to have called the offensive in Afghanistan the 'equivalent of Mike Tyson in the ring with a five-year-old child...'[8]. These comparisons are patently unfair in the sense that this five-year-old child, the Islamist terrorists, who carried out the strikes on USA in September 2001, knew what they were about. The USA is actually carrying a sledgehammer to swat a fly. The sledgehammer is far too unwieldy. It destroys the masonry wherever it lands. The ferocity of the bin Laden orchestrated attacks in USA would suggest a personal revenge motive. Was bin Laden short-changed by the CIA or the US oil interests? The truth will not be out. The Pakistani generals, while publicly embracing the Americans – no matter how uncomfortable the embrace – are busy hedging their bets whenever the opportunity to do so presents itself.

The Americans have compounded their difficulties in other spheres as well. The September 11 attacks showed up American vulnerabilities. It demonstrated that for a full 24 hours the decision-making apparatus of the mighty first power of the world had been paralyzed. The myth of invincibility lay shattered. As if that were not enough a feeling has been allowed to grow around the world that the high-tech warriors have no stomach for man-to-man close quarter battle, which is the *sine qua non* for fighting terrorists in any part of the world. This works to USA's disadvantage in several ways. To begin with the US public and the US government have themselves become stultified into this pattern of this thinking; the US army has gone overboard in its belief that high-tech is a panacea for every type of fighting. As a result of the mentality that this belief induced in the country it is possible that the rank and file of the US military have psychologically, if not physically, conditioned themselves into such thinking. The demonstrated inability to take casualties emboldens the adversaries.

Of the three countries responsible for the genesis of the global *jehad* factories now in peak production modes, USA played the role of a catalyst. It played chaplain to the marriage of the Islamic clergy in an unholy alliance with the Pakistan military to progress the US Cold War aims against the Soviet occupation forces in Afghanistan. Saudi Arabia provided the financing. As the principal cold warrior of the Western alliance, the USA could not have been faulted for trying to undermine the spread of Soviet influence and as a result, of communist expansion. After the Soviet withdrawal the US did not lose interest in the region as such; it became preoccupied with the decline in the US economy and the greater decline in the fortunes of the military-industrial complex at the end of the Cold War. Miraculously, an unexpected opportunity appeared in the guise of their erstwhile ally, Saddam Hussein who was casting covetous glances at the oil reserves of his neighbour Kuwait in order to recover from the massive setback to the Iraqi economy during the Iran-Iraq war. Whether Saddam Hussein was 'set up' or given the wrong signals by the US State department before embarking on his invasion of Kuwait will remain a matter of speculation till more definitive inputs are available from either the Iraqis in the know or the principal US actors of that time.

The Iraqi action led to the Gulf War. Automatically US attention shifted to the new theater of war and Afghanistan was put on the back burner.

While the USA and its Western allies were fully occupied with the Gulf War and the post-Gulf War strategies for restoring the fortunes of the military-industrial complex on the one hand and destroying Iraq's residual military potential in the WMD domain on the other, Pakistan used the opportunity to refashion Afghanistan in its own image. It is not as if the USA did not know what was going on. It is that it cynically sought to exploit the opportunity presented by the Taliban expansion in Afghanistan to further its own oil strategy for the region at the cost of Iran, Russia and China. Therefore, while Pakistan concentrated on creating its strategic depth in Afghanistan, to be followed with a strategic link up with US oil interests in Central Asia, the USA started dreaming of a Central Command bestriding the oil wealth of the Middle East *and* Central Asia. The Americans were not fully conscious of the fact that China had similar designs through its growing alliance with Pakistan, and through them the Taliban. So confident was China of its ability to outsmart USA that it became incautious enough to transfer nuclear and missile high-tech to Pakistan. Neither China nor the USA realised that Pakistan was developing its own potential to be the ultimate arbiter in the Great Game. Had the situation developed according to plan Pakistan would have strengthened its nuclear arsenal and delivery systems in time frames that matched Taliban's ingress into Central Asia, after over-running the Northern Alliance. At that stage, Pakistan would have been able to barter Central Asia's oil exit routes between the major global players. So thought the Pakistan generals. The countries that would have suffered from this development would generally have been Iran and Russia. It is not inconceivable that the

Taliban may have nurtured its own strategy for Central Asia and Pakistan. It could have been at variance with the strategy of the Pakistan generals.

Whatever be the case, it was a classic case of strategic overreach by Pakistan. The strategy being adopted by the Pakistan military paid no heed to the threats that could emerge to Pakistan from a failed strategy. Nor were they mindful of the precarious nature of the Pakistan economy. Had the US been even peripherally alert to the developments in Pakistan and Afghanistan it would have been spared the traumas of the September 11 events. Added to their own ostrich-like policy in this regard they failed to heed the warnings sent to them by others, including the Indian government. Their intelligence agencies failed to read the signs coming loud and clear from the Pakistan–Afghanistan cauldron, for several reasons. The most important reason was that during the period from 1980-1989 when they were backing the military government of General Zia-ul-Haq to the hilt they allowed the Pakistan ISI and bin Laden and his close operatives deep insights into the functioning of the CIA. The intimacy developed between the CIA and the ISI and its operatives in Afghanistan under the direct patronage of the then CIA chief was of a nature that it created future vulnerabilities for the USA. Simply stated, the US establishment and its global agencies went overboard on Pakistan. They threw caution to the winds. Today the knowledge that many operatives in the ISI and Al Qaeda – both interchangeable – have of the functioning of CIA and many of its top operatives, who were field officers and middle ranking operatives at that time, is such that they are able to anticipate CIA actions at least three moves ahead.

That is not all. It is very much possible that in the bonhomie created at that time, bin Laden and the ISI were used to carry out clandestine activities on behalf of the CIA, that is to say USA, against third countries and even friendly countries where the CIA did not want to dirty its hands. It is also possible that these elements were used to further the economic interests of several powerful groups in the US industry and government. Many of those people would be in the top echelons of the US government and industry today. It would not be easy for the US establishment to sever all those linkages as cleanly as they would wish. The blackmail potential of the ISI – Al Qaeda – bin Laden triad cannot be ruled out. For a long time to come the US government will remain hostage to its dirty manoeuvers of yesteryear.

Barely ten years after leaving the theatre the USA is back with a vengeance. Unbelievably, it actually expected the ISI to handcuff itself and surrender to the US Sherrif. There can be no greater form of naïveté. The US establishment is still having difficulty in appreciating that bin Laden, Al Qaeda and the ISI are one and the same thing. The pound of flesh that the US extracts from the Pakistan general at the top is given back by the ISI operatives to the Taliban at the field level. - the business end, the operating end. In one form or the other the US is in for the long haul. Having established a military presence in the subcontinent and Central Asia it has already set its sights – ably assisted by the British – on becoming the successor in the 21st century to their colonial cousins of the 19th century (and first half of the 20th century). Times have changed. The Pax Americana is not the same thing as the Pax Britannica of another era. The Americans may not have had a choice but to pick up the gauntlet thrown at them in New York and Washington on September 11, 2001. In the fight against global terror the world instinctively and unstintingly rallied behind them in their hour of grief. The mourning for the dead is over. There are apprehensions that under the guise of bringing bin Laden and Al Qaeda to book the Americans may be cynically exploiting the world's sympathetic response for grander designs to bolster their role as the remaining superpower of the world. The people of America should take heed. What their government may be attempting to do over and beyond the need for bringing the culprits of the dark deeds to book may be a clear case of strategic overreach – even for America.

The Increasing Planetary Stresses

Newspaper and television channels are full of tales of collateral damage caused by intense US bombing in Afghanistan. Stories of human misery and civilian casualties abound. Tragically, not much heed has been given to the ecological devastation that is proceeding apace by the use of the most lethal and devastating explosive materials being employed from the most technically advanced arsenal in the world to flush out adversaries from their mountain strongholds. Both sides appear to be oblivious – uncaring as well – to the harm being done; one side by using the centuries old water channels, the irrigation lifeline of Afghanistan, to escape detection, and the other side in destroying them to flush out their adversaries. Statements were made that should the 5000 pound, below ground penetrating bombs not give the desired results, tactical, low yield, nuclear weapons could be considered. Their use was not categorically ruled out. What the world does not realize – and those in the know choose to remain silent – is that in all likelihood depleted uranium penetrators are being used to target some of the more impregnable cavern defences. More lethal forms of munitions would also be in the process of being tried out, without let or hindrance, till the manufacturers are satisfied as to their accuracy and effect - for future conflicts. Afghanistan is the perfect proving ground, perhaps the most ideal in the world. For a long time to come it will remain in the control of the Taliban or their successors and the US and their allies, both local and global. Till well into the new century no one will be allowed to make a survey of the ecological devastation knowingly visited on that hapless country. The water channels will end up by being contaminated with radioactive materials with half-life, like depleted uranium, counted in hundreds of million and billions of years. Who can tell how many generations of Afghans will suffer from genetic modification, sterility and a host of associated mutations. It is for the public in Pakistan and the US public to realize that what was undertaken in their names by their governments over the previous decades is permanently destroying a global habitat. A part of the planet is being irreversibly destroyed. Whether humans are found inside or not the use of fuel air explosives near the cave of a mouth or inside the cave will collapse the lungs, breathing apparatus and sensors of trillions of life forms living in that cave since time immemorial, since well before humans made their appearance on the planet. No matter which side wins, a terrible tragedy is unfolding before mankind. Stupidly, insanely, every country – actually the leadership of these countries – still continue to talk of geo-strategic advantages. Irreversible damage is being done to the flora and fauna of the region. Avifaunal winter migration across the Eurasian landmass will be severely affected, leading to a global decline in many species already on the endangered list. The excerpts taken from a report sent by a NGO to the UN Secretary General during the bombing of Yugoslavia and a UN committee report need to be taken note of by the global community for carrying out urgent studies on the ecological consequences of renewed military activity of the super high-tech variety.

"Through explosive reactions, fires and the burning of great amounts of different materials and chemicals and through intensive actions of military airplanes, the millions of tons of oxygen that the living world needs, have been irretrievably spent." [9]

Very obviously, in spite of the alarm bells ringing from every corner of the globe on the dangerous levels of eco-destruction taking place, the military-industrial complex of the major powers show scant regard for such concerns. The increasing reliance on electronics in the so-called RMA is slowly destroying the life support sensory abilities of the myriad life forms inhabiting the planet. The world seems to have become oblivious to the needs of the other species. Soon enough it would become clear to every human being that today: "The dangers that the world faces from eco-destruction of the planet dwarf the mere problems of national security".

Indo-Afghan Relations

India had a very deep, traditional relationship with Afghanistan in the earlier decades after independence. The mutual understanding that had developed was good for both countries as well as the region. It was a period of relative calm. People of India and Afghanistan, possibly others as well, look upon the period with nostalgia. It has vanished like a dream, perhaps never to return in the lifetime of the generations that witnessed the good days. Unfortunately, it was the superpower rivalry during the Cold War accompanied by a desire by Pakistan, at some stage, to directly interfere in the affairs of its western neighbour that brought instability to Afghanistan, followed by a long spell of turmoil and uncertainty. Nobody can tell when peace will return to that troubled country.

The most unfortunate part of the tragedy in Afghanistan is the mistrust that has developed between the people of Afghanistan and almost all the countries in its neighbourhood. To begin with Russia is mistrusted. India lost the gratitude and friendship of the Afghan people due to its lack of condemnation of the Soviet occupation and its tacit, albeit reluctant, acceptance. Pakistan had emerged as a friendly country till it overplayed its hand due to the ambitions of the Pakistani generals. Today a stage has been reached such that Pakistan is perhaps more hated by the bulk of the people in Afghanistan than any other country in Afghan history of the last century. The Central Asian countries mistrust the majority Pushtuns, as do the Iranians. The Americans will continue to be despised by Pushtuns in Afghanistan and the Muslims in general, for a long time to come. India not having geographical contiguity and being denied access by Pakistan can only rebuild its bridges on the coat tails of the Russians, Iranians, the CAR and the Northern Alliance. It will take enormous patience and political sagacity for it to reestablish a significant presence in Afghanistan.

India would need to strengthen its intelligence operations in the entire Central Asian region and the Middle East. It has to pay special attention to radical Islamist elements exfiltrating from Afghanistan–Pakistan to lie low in India and Bangladesh. If not anticipated and neutralised the threat posed by these elements in the long-term could become formidable. Narcotics traffic to and through India could increase due to the US intervention in Afghanistan. It is estimated that Afghanistan's opium crop of 3.656 metric tonnes accounted for 72 per cent of the world's illicit opium in 2000. Since 1997, over 96 per cent of the opium-poppy crop has been cultivated in Taliban controlled areas. Opium-poppy cultivation in Afghanistan continues to increase, despite a devastating drought and decrees from the Taliban leadership banning poppy cultivation.[10]

India's policy toward Afghanistan has lacked clarity and purpose since the Soviet occupation of Afghanistan that the government of India felt obliged to accept; in spite of New Delhi's misgivings on an issue of vital concern to India. Thereafter, the country's policy toward Kabul has been hostage to its relations with Pakistan. It has been predicated reactively to Pakistan's actions in Afghanistan. India's traditional friendship with Afghanistan was wrenchingly disrupted when the Soviet forces marched into Afghanistan in 1979. For the next quarter century India's Afghan policy drifted along in an uncertain manner. At the present juncture India, lacking any real hold or ability to influence matters, can only watch helplessly as Afghanistan fractures into zones of influence. Should this trend continue it amounts to a *de facto* break up or partition of Afghanistan on the lines of the partitioning of India at the time of the departure of the British. When that happens it would be naïve for India to blame the global powers for Afghanistan's break up. Afghanistan's misfortune cannot be laid at Russia or America's door. Afghanistan's troubles were cannily built into the post-World War II grand design of Britain when the colonial power partitioned India on the basis of religion before leaving the subcontinent. Britain is not entirely to blame either. Full 50 years elapsed before the events that shaped the terrible Afghan tragedy of the closing years of the 20th century and beginning of the next. The tragedy of Afghanistan can be laid at the door of Pakistan and India, in that order. Had these two nations buried their differences after the Soviet departure, no third country could ever have ventured into any part of the subcontinent, from Colombo to Kabul. Looking ahead, if there has to be a mitigation of the Afghan tragedy and amelioration of the condition of the Afghan people, a rosier future can only take shape if Pakistan and India sink their differences and jointly work for the stability and well being of Afghanistan.

7

September 11 Events: Global Perspective

Even if peace is restored and major conflagrations do not take place it will take a generation for the scars to heal and for mutual suspicions to melt away. Global perceptions that have radically altered for a large percentage of people in the countries most affected are tabulated below:

> Americans will never again feel safe in several predominantly Muslim countries. US officials working in Muslim countries will generally reside behind barricades or electronic surveillance (as was the case in Iran during the regime of the Shah in the build up to the Khomeini revolution).
>
> The picture of American irrationality in targeting all South Asian and other non-white foreigners consequent to the collapse of the twin towers will remain etched in the minds of the victim communities for a long time to come. While young people may continue to flock to the US, the more adult, self-respecting Asians are bound to have second thoughts. For a few mesmerising days the veneer of civilisation disappeared from the face of the most advanced civilisation in the world. The Americans could unflinchingly inflict pain on others. But the upholders of morality and cherished American values were unable to take pain. (It should be mentioned, however, that the immediate

- response to a similar outrage in several other countries of the world might possibly have been more savage).
- Hereafter, the Atlantic and Pacific Oceans no longer confer immunity on the USA.
- The world – and many thinking Americans – perceived that US security lies in global security and not in *high-tech planet destroying warfare*. Whether the US government comes round to this point of view will decide, to a large extent, the direction the world takes in the coming years. (The European allies of the US must exert themselves to propel the US in this direction for the benefit of the Western alliance and the world in general).
- Ironically – and perhaps tragically – the twin towers attack has helped to consolidate the hold in the US of the very forces that were the most hated face of America *for the elements* that carried out the attack. President George W Bush and the extreme right in US politics have been strengthened immeasurably.
- The Anglo-American media played an important role in whipping up war hysteria and hard line opinion moulding.
- The enduring nature of the Anglo-American entente has again been demonstrated. Britain has emerged as the key player for the furtherance of US interests in the area of the Great Game of 19th and 20th centuries. Regardless of all else, the Anglo-American forces will remain a presence in the region for the foreseeable future.

Reformulating the Ground Rules For Combating Global Terrorism

If terrorism is a global menace then global protocols to fight terrorism should gradually replace US-centric understandings arrived at bilaterally between USA and various countries and groupings.

A minimum common global platform should include:

(a) Elimination of nuclear/WMD capacity of states capable of sponsoring terrorism. Short-term agreements are no substitute for long-term guarantees. Hence 'extinguishment' of capability becomes an overriding priority. Concomitant cutting back of the arsenals of the P5 (permanent) nuclear weapon states as a prelude to complete nuclear disarmament.

(b) The US should use the opportunity for harmonization with global community.

(c) The US to defer/renounce NMD.

(d) Strengthening the UN. Without a strengthened UN system that is seen to be fair by all nations, no lasting solution to the problem would be possible.

(e) Countries retaliating against state–sponsored WTC type strikes anywhere in the world, to be guaranteed immunity against WMD/nuclear retaliation from states nurturing terrorism when undertaking US type hot pursuit or other retaliatory measures - confined to attacks against terrorist networks only.

(f) All WTC type of terrorist attacks to be construed as attacks against humanity or the comity of nations.

Islam Linked to Terror

Some time toward the end of September 2001 an article in the *Daily Telegraph* of London carried the headline: "a religion that sanctions violence". Without putting too fine a construction on it, it can be said that, rightly or wrongly, Islam *has* become synonymous with terror in recent years. It had come to the fore well before Samuel Huntington's theories on the 'Clash of Civilisations' had become known to the world at large. The debate has become infructuous and unnecessary. Bringing in theology merely plays into the hands of the interested groups on both sides of the divide. The bare truth is far more simple and uncomplicated. It so happens that in the second half of the 20th century the Middle East came into prominence on account of its oil and the rising oil prices that brought in tremendous wealth to the nations in the Middle East blessed with large oil reserves. It also came into public consciousness on account of the Palestinian problem and the Khomeini revolution in Iran. It so happened that all the concerned countries were Muslim countries. Thereafter, the Iran-Iraq war followed by the Gulf War were both fought in the Middle East; in a theatre that was entirely peopled by Muslims. The invaders who came in to restore the balance and pumped in the armaments to create the next imbalance were all non-Muslims. Historically, the wealth of nations and technological superiority had generally passed into the hands of the developed nations in the West. They were all Christians. So whether the fight was over territory, territorial aggrandizement, or the creation and cornering of wealth, the parties involved were Muslim countries on one side and countries that were predominantly Christian on the other. It just happened that way. If there had not been such large reserves of oil in the Middle East on which the industrialized world became so dependent nobody would have given a second thought to the Muslim world. Again, it is simply happenstance that oil was discovered in such abundance in a region that had been the battle ground between Christianity and Islam for nearly a millennium. By the same token, in another fifty years when the oil is depleted or when alternate sources of energy are found the terror linked to Islam and the clash of civilizations would have become a distant memory.

Large influx of wealth creates its own dynamic. Wealthy nations wish to become militarily powerful, not necessarily to conquer other nations. Many of them wish to merely protect their wealth. In the present case it was the largesse dispensed by Saudi Arabia to a very willing and penurious Pakistan to do their bidding that created much of the turmoil in the region, and beyond. Not having popular support, the reigning regimes in both countries, Saudi Arabia and Pakistan, decided to keep the clergy on their side. It should have been anticipated that a stage would come when the clergy, sensing the nearness of political power, would not be content to play second fiddle. Since the clergy would not have been allowed to raise military forces or subordinate the established military hierarchy to their will, they decided to take the route of the seminaries to project their power on to the national and then international scene. At this stage Islam and terror became synonymous. It had nothing to do with Huntington and the West.

Turkey, successor of the Ottoman Empire, was modernised by Kemal Ataturk. He decided to abolish the Caliphate instead of trying to reform it. He gave the new republic a good foundation, a solid scientific structure, modern education and a new direction. Except for Turkey the Muslims of the Middle East generally remained trapped in the Middle Ages. With unequal distribution of wealth, lack of modern health and education facilities many people in these countries sensed that in one way or the other the world was passing them by. It bred resentment. The Western nations were perceived to be the exploiters. They *were* the exploiters. A clash was inevitable. When it came it surprised everyone with its vigour and intensity. It is just the beginning. Call it a civilisation clash or Islamic terror. It will continue till some redistribution of wealth takes place between the exploiters and the exploited.

Another way out of the predicament is for the intellectuals in the Islamic world to push for modern education and better governance in their respective countries. More than a century earlier Meiji Japan had demonstrated that education provided young people with the opportunity to move out of the conditions into which they were born. The same has been demonstrated time and again in the 20th century in many parts of the world. Societies that were not afraid of change and went out of their way to embrace change moved ahead to blossom forth in their own country and to leave their mark on the countries to which they migrated. It is indeed unfortunate that as a civilization, as a territorial grouping, as a religious insularity, the Muslim countries turned their back on change and modernisation. Unless they seize the opportunity to dispassionately look within and reexamine their present state and the direction in which they are headed they will sink deeper into the morass of backwardness. No amount of terror or apportioning of blame on the outsiders will ameliorate their condition. From out of the Afghan tragedy many of them are being afforded the chance to break the shackles of their societal enslavement at the hands of obscurantist elements in their own countries. They should seize the opportunity with both hands.

The terror attacks on the USA are the early manifestation of a much deeper ferment that could keep exploding volcanically in many parts of the world, under varying circumstances. The internal conditions in almost all the Islamic countries are becoming worse with each passing year. While the rest of the world moved into the new century many Islamic societies reversed direction to march backwards into the centuries gone by. The chronological incongruity introduces a fundamental incompatibility between them and societies that have modernized. The aftermath of the September 11 disaster and the certainty of US retaliation has led to some form of churning in almost all countries with large Muslim populations, regardless of how far away they happen to be from the epicenter of the retaliatory US actions. The unrest – in many cases unease – is being exploited by forces that are inimical to USA and the West as also to the governing hierarchies in their own countries. The fault line that is developing across the Muslim world is not so much mere political unrest; it is in the nature of a rebellion against their lot and a feeling of helplessness against an inability to improve their lot under the existing global dispensation.

The manner in which the discontent is being exploited by one set of people or being dealt with by another is true to form. The first lot is attempting to channelise the unrest into a more regressive form of politico-religious orthodoxy. The other side representing the established order knows only of one way of dealing with the situation. More force. Unless a way is found to discard both the extremes, Muslim societies will continue to explode or implode. Either way the repercussions of the explosion - or implosion - will continue to be felt in the rest of the world.

The WTC attacks that led to the US intervention in Afghanistan have released forces around the world that may be difficult to control until a global consensus, preferably under a strengthened and impartial United Nations, is arrived at. The US bombings of Afghanistan have been ferocious, the ferocity heightened by the elusive nature of the opponents. Shadowy figures that can melt away into the mountains, slink in with the refugees, hide in the mosques, or simply disappear into the adjoining areas of Pakistan. Till an accommodation is arrived at, or victory achieved, the bombings could continue with increased civilian casualties by way of collateral damage. Here cause and effect take over. The prolonged bombings arouse disquiet around the world. In predominantly Muslim countries, especially Indonesia, the Arab world and Pakistan, street processions and clashes with the police can provide a safety valve for the anger welling up. The problem arises for the Muslim populations that have migrated to the West, notably USA and UK, the two countries at the forefront of the initiative for the global response to counter terrorism. These two countries are the ones physically involved in the military action in Afghanistan. The Muslim populations of USA and UK who are against the continued bombing in Afghanistan cannot be part of organised protests as these would be construed by the governments of their countries - and the white population at large - as hostile acts or acts of disloyalty.

The Muslims in these countries are already under suspicion. By public denunciation of the actions of their governments they can only add to their problems. In the UK some of the Muslims have left to go and join the *jehad* against the military interventions. There is talk that the people who have gone to fight in Afghanistan from the UK against their own country's intervention could have committed treason. Whether a case of treason can be upheld in a court of law - since Britain has not declared war on Afghanistan as such - could become the center point of a fierce debate on the subject. The problem that has surfaced does not end there. What about the rest of the Muslim population that has taken up British citizenship or US citizenship? Should the relatives of the people who have gone to fight in Afghanistan, on the wrong side so to say, be included in the circle of suspicion? Would they become automatic targets of government surveillance? Would jobs be denied to them? What about schooling and housing in mixed neighbourhoods?

Had an incident of this nature occurred after a few generations it would not have mattered very much. By that time assimilation would have taken place, to a large extent. The question of divided loyalties would not have arisen. In the present turmoil assimilation has not taken place. The Muslim communities are sticking together in a clannish fashion. Their links with the countries from which they migrated are deeper than the links with their adopted countries. They have left behind several close relations. In many cases parents, sisters and brothers. On an emotional plane, their response as a community is understandable. An objective outsider could sympathise with it, even empathise.

In the conflict that could follow, with its global dimensions, the reaction of the Muslim communities in the West is bound to lead to greater societal cleavages, that might not be restricted to cleavage between the Muslim community and the whites. It could extend to schisms between other non-white communities, following different religions. Very few people from the non-Muslim countries had left their countries to go and settle in Muslim countries in the past. It is unlikely that many non-Muslims would wish to transplant themselves to live in Muslim countries in the future. They would not be able to adjust to the medieval practices in vogue in most of these countries. Migrations in the 20th century after World War II have generally been from the Muslim countries to India (from Pakistan and Bangladesh well after independence) and to the West. Followers of *jehad* advocated by the radical Islamic movements, coming to the fore in Pakistan and Afghanistan, never stop to think of the damage that they would be doing to millions of their fellow Muslims settled in the West by taking up *jehad* against USA. By committing these atrocities they have condemned their fellow Muslims who had sought refuge in the West, from persecution or for bettering their lot, to a life of suspicion and discrimination. In the process they may have put a stop to future migrations.

Muslims in Pakistan and elsewhere, rallying to the *jehadi* banner, may not be aware that China - even China - the trusted friend of Pakistan, had barred citizens of 20 countries from traveling on its airlines, fearing attacks of the type that resulted in the September 11 suicide missions in the United States. The list included Afghanistan, Algeria, Bahrain, Egypt, Iran, Iraq, Israel, Jordan, Kuwait, Lebanon, Oman, *Pakistan*, Qatar, Syria, Saudi Arabia, Sudan and the United Arab Emirates. Interestingly, the list excludes the Muslim majority countries of South East Asia because, in the Chinese perception, they represent people from composite cultures. India and countries like India with varied ethnicities, languages and religion are the true laboratories of composite culture that need to be preserved - and strengthened – by the people of India and all countries on the subcontinent. It is in everyone's interest to do so.

Subcontinental Fallout

The continuing civil war in Afghanistan, fuelled through external interventions, represented a major challenge to the security environment of the region. The outside interventions introduced newer weapons into the theatre and ended up by weaponising the whole region at a much higher level of across the board lethality. In the first decade after the Soviet withdrawal the impact of the continued fighting in Afghanistan was felt mostly in Pakistan and the immediate neighbourhood. What the world failed to realize was that the pattern of schooling, indoctrination and training being imparted in the seminaries in Pakistan was bound to have a global impact sooner or later. USA, and much of the world that had the ability and wherewithal to do something about the situation, were remiss in under-estimating the expanding nature of the threat that it posed to the global fraternity. Something akin to September 11 was waiting to happen. The surprise is that it took so long to happen and the form in which it finally happened.

Even now the outside forces that have intervened in Afghanistan do not appear to fully comprehend the nature of Afghan society. It is worth recalling what an Englishman wrote about the Afghan people a long while ago:

> *"The nation consists of a mere collection of tribes, of unequal powers and divergent habits, which are held together, more or less closely, according to the personal character of the Chief who rules them. The feeling of patriotism, as known in Europe, cannot exist among the Afghans, for there is no common country. In its place is found a strong turbulent love of individual liberty, which naturally rebels against authority, and would be impatient of control, whether exercised by Russians, English, Persians or even Durranis".* [11]
>
> **... Sir Henry Rawlinson**

It is pertinent to recall that for nearly a thousand years most of the kings who sat on the throne of Delhi came from Afghanistan and Central Asia. The successful invasions of Afghanistan itself have generally come from across the Hindukush. The attempts by the armies of the Sikh Maharaja Ranjit Singh and the British never really succeeded in their hegemonist designs. Historically then, it would appear that it has been far easier for invaders to come *down* into the plains of North India than the reverse proposition. Pakistan forgot the lesson of history; and by its India-centric fixation imperiled its future by venturing into Afghanistan as king makers and future handlers of the rulers of Kabul. The primary source of discord between Afghanistan and Pakistan has been the Pushtuns living in the border areas astride the Durand Line. While the Pakistan government has been laying claims to these areas on a geographic basis, the Afghanistan governments lay claim on the entire Pushtun population due to its Afghan origin i.e., on grounds of ethnicity. The Pakistan generals used the pretext of the Soviet invasion to resolve the Pushtun issue and the problem of the Durand Line by attempting to extend their reach up to Kabul and beyond. They tried to make Afghanistan a tributary of Pakistan. In the process the entire region is in turmoil. A probable outcome could be the creation of Pakhtoonistan incorporating areas in both Afghanistan and across the Durand Line in Pakistan. It is for the people of Pakistan to realize that the Pakistan military, and its extension the ISI, have played Russian roulette with the future of Pakistan, unbeknownst to the people of Pakistan, and quite often without the knowledge of the Pakistan military hierarchy itself. Therefore, unless a full-fledged democratic government is restored in Pakistan with adequate safeguards against military coups, further breakup of Pakistan could well be on the cards.

There have been unintended effects of the September 11 events. These rebounded indiscriminately on several Asian societies who had neither the knowledge of what was going to happen, nor would have approved what happened in America on that fateful day. An immediate response to the September 11 attacks was the harassment and victimization of people of South Asian origin in the US. Anger and fear came together to evoke a pattern of responses that could not have been justified then, or later on when the anger had subsided and the fear brought under control. While many people privately agonized over these basic instincts having taken over, there remained in their midst sizeable numbers in whom xenophobic tendencies came to the fore. They are likely to remain there for a long time to come.

South Asians continue to be targeted. While the anger is specifically directed at Muslims and their countries of origin many more people from the region, belonging to different faiths, were victimized and may continue to be victimised. Segregation in mixed neighbourhoods might take place; with the authorities looking the other way. Many of the elements that made American society unique may change, perhaps forever. Asian mothers, especially from South Asia and the Muslim countries, will worry more about racial attacks on their children.

People will instinctively start classifying other people whom they see at airports, on trains, in buses and restaurants by racial types. 'They' and 'us' will become extenuated. If the other person is one of 'us' a relaxed smile may appear. If the person does not fall into the 'us' category the guard may remain up. Spontaneous bonhomie may not return any time soon in America. The natural tendency would be to blame American society for their lack of tolerance. Few people, especially the victims of racial prejudice, will think of blaming their plight on the terrorists who carried out the attacks.

The worst victims of racial prejudice in the years ahead could be Pakistanis who might still want to migrate to other countries of the world. They too might blame their misfortune on the racial prejudice of the Western world. What is taking place in America is spreading to the rest of Europe and to other countries. Not many years ago, taking it out on South Asians was referred to as 'Paki bashing'. The phenomenon, while it had not entirely disappeared, had nearly died down. It may return in a far more virulent form. Not only will the Pakistani people be detested in many parts of the world, they would, in a way have been responsible for subjecting the other South Asians to 'Paki bashing' as well. What will be the outcome of all this? Will it lead to greater understanding and harmonisation between the countries of the subcontinent or will it extend the religious divide and burnish communalism? Everybody looks to India to demonstrate the efficacy of a pluralist society. Before that happens Pakistan too will have to make amends. Not to India, but to itself. When Pakistan was formed the non-Muslim minorities constituted nearly 17 percent of the population. Their numbers have dwindled drastically. Those that still remain are subjected to harsh restrictions and the blasphemy laws. Unless the average citizen of Pakistan rediscovers the true face of Islam and welcomes back his brethren from the other communities – all from the same racial stock on the subcontinent – the state of Pakistan will continue to go downhill, regardless of the largesse it receives from donors in the West, who have been exploiting the country for their own ends. In this hour of reckoning for Pakistan a new opportunity has been given to the people of Pakistan to rediscover themselves and their true heritage.

Non-Muslims have been described in the Shari'ah as *zimmis*. Islamic regimes are enjoined to look after the welfare of the *zimmis* who are part of its responsibility. The Prophet's sayings have it that those who neglect *zimmis* will not be from his *ummah* and, therefore, they will not be able to join him and his band of followers on the Day of Judgment. Hence, looking after the welfare of non-Muslims is a responsibility of the Islamic state, which it sheds at its peril. Islamic governments and people who support them i.e., the ordinary Muslims of an Islamic state cannot aspire for the benevolence of His Prophet or for the Mercy of Allah if they oppress the non-Muslim people in their state. In Pakistan, as well as Bangladesh, such oppression is rampant. It is endemic. Neither the government nor the citizens of these countries have a right to call themselves true Muslims. By abdicating their primary responsibility these states, as per the very scriptures that they never fail to quote, are knowingly putting themselves beyond the Islamic pale by their harsh edicts against non-Muslims. They are putting themselves into grave moral degeneration, as their actions are at variance with the finest tenets of Islam.

They must objectively examine the personality of the Taliban leaders who narrowly interpret obscure medieval texts and apply them unthinkingly to living human beings, without being in a position to examine their relevance. These leaders, who have come to the fore through violence and terror, have never had an exposure to any humanizing or ennobling ideas that scholars, philosophers and saints of all religions throughout the ages have delved into to arrive at more humane, tolerant and compassionate worldviews. If not the radicalized products of *madrasas*, at least the rest of the people in Pakistan should be able to ponder whether governance in the world of the 21st century can be based on items lifted out of context from rule books written centuries ago.

At several levels there is a desire in the Pakistan society, almost a pathetic craving, to interact with the modern world, especially the Western world, otherwise so many of their people would not have attempted to migrate abroad. Even now, if the state of Pakistan does not collapse upon itself like the twin towers, it will be on account of help extended to it by the international community. Nobody in Pakistan seems to be rejecting this help. It is eagerly solicited. Should that be the case, the very basis of the term *zimmi* loses its relevance. Human rights now enjoy universal acceptance, at least in principle. Equality before the law is the basis of every modern state. The Taliban leaders, and leaders like them surfacing elsewhere in the world, not having had any meaningful interaction with the outside world, have no understanding of modern societies and the global interdependence that is being forced upon mankind in the new world order; or the planetary stresses that threaten the future of the human race. Which rational being can really attempt to justify that obscurantist leaders like the Taliban, steeped in medieval theocracy, should be at the helm of the affairs in any country.

The true greatness of any humanist, the world over, lay in the person's compassion, which is born through sensitivity to the suffering of others. Compassion is the true spiritual quality. It embraces all humans, all God's creatures. There is no human being who does not suffer. There is no living creature that does not suffer. Humans and creation are bound to each other through compassion and love. Any religious person should be devoted above all to the removal of suffering. The religious leader who is not sensitive to the suffering of all humans, be they men, women or children, can have no claim to spirituality. People with compassion will not be immune to suffering, injustice, or any inequality that incites hatred and leads to suffering. It is axiomatic that individuals imbued with compassion are by their very nature tolerant of the foibles, weaknesses and beliefs of others. Lack of compassion and tolerance and consequent increase of hatred in any society will result in the breakdown of that society.

China

Many people - outside Pakistan and Afghanistan - had started becoming apprehensive at the type of technology transfers that China was making to its Pakistan allies. It was consciously abetting the strengthening of the Pakistan nuclear arsenal and the delivery systems, notably the longer-range missiles. It had made overtures to the Taliban from the outset, possibly to build bridges with the new order taking shape in Afghanistan and perhaps to limit the help being extended to the Uighur separatist elements in Xinjiang. There had been disturbing reports appearing from time to time of increasing economic and security ties between China and the Taliban. Most people did not discount them because it appeared to be a natural extension of help being extended by China to Taliban's creators, the Pakistan military and the ISI. Deeper linkages could have been in the offing between Beijing, Islamabad, Kabul, and on to Central Asia, following in the wake of the Taliban's northward thrust. It is not entirely dissimilar to what the US is now attempting to do from another direction – Washington, London, Islamabad, Kabul, Tashkent and on to the rest of Central Asia. Russia is poised delicately between these two geo-strategic thrust lines, one from the East and the other from the West. The first one temporarily suppressed, possibly going into a state of dormancy, the latter in its hyper active stage. India, Iran and Russia could play a moderating role to roll back both these extra territorial urges, to provide breathing space to Central Asia and, at a later stage to Afghanistan, Pakistan and the rest of South Asia. It needs to be added here that the Chinese initiatives towards the Taliban included training for Taliban forces in Chinese training centers, direct flights between Urumchi and Kabul, and arms supplies to the Taliban, paid for by the narcotics profits made by the Taliban.

Immediately after the September 11 attacks, China, like the rest of the world, supported US initiatives to fight global terrorism. There was not much ambiguity in the quickness or quality of the response. Doubtless, the Chinese would have let it be known that USA would be expected to tone down its rhetoric and support for Taiwan and Tibet. However, as the Anglo-American designs for post-Taliban strategies in Central Asia started to become clearer China had second thoughts on the subject.

The (Propagandistic) Apotheosis of the Taliban

The Taliban were actually losing ground and quite rapidly at that. Before the September 11 events and the US response to those events people in Afghanistan were getting fed up with the archaic restrictions imposed by the Taliban. These restrictions had begun to horrify the average Pakistani and Muslims elsewhere on the subcontinent. On the ground itself while the Taliban claimed to be in control of over 90 per cent of Afghan territory, in reality their control was mainly over the cities and towns. They did not have similar control over the countryside. There would have been a likelihood that in a few years the Taliban would have been overthrown or pushed back territorially. Pakistan society itself was getting alarmed at the reverse flow into Pakistan of the Taliban influence.

September 11 changed everything, more so for the principle actors, the Taliban, Pakistan, Saudi Arabia and USA. Initially the Taliban and their supporters in Pakistan and Afghanistan were taken aback at the cold fury that seemed to be rising in America in the aftermath of the WTC and Pentagon attacks. It was felt that the US reactions would be swift and extraordinarily severe. As the days passed by the US began to put together global support for their fight against terrorism. It also needed time to complete its deployment and build up logistic support for its retaliatory actions. This period of approximately 3 to 4 weeks gave the Taliban sufficient time to readjust their positions and to analyze the likely pattern of the US response. It also gave the Pakistan army generals and the ISI sufficient time to re-supply the Taliban and provide them with fresh inputs that could help them to withstand the American response when it materialized. All this while the Pakistan head of state and the military top brass were being railroaded into accepting American military deployment on the territory of Pakistan. The vital clues that were essential for the Taliban's strategy to counter the US retaliation was the appreciation that coordination with the Northern Alliance was only superficial and that the US ground forces would not come into play in any meaningful strength for quite some time. These inputs were crucial for the redeployments that were effected by the Taliban. In some respects the game was given away even before the battle was joined.

There is no gainsaying that the Taliban (and the term includes the Taliban associate bin Laden) suffered considerable casualties and equipment losses due to the US bombing. However, there was a trade-off taking place. Whatever was being lost by way of heavy equipment was being more than made up by way of increase in their manpower strength, and the opposition to US bombings in the entire Muslim world. It helped in many ways. The most important aspect was that temporarily it pushed in the background Taliban's crimes against women and their image for barbarism. Almost overnight the word Taliban became a generic term for anti-US resistance. The Taliban cleverly co-opted the anti-US feeling into its response to US intervention in Afghanistan. Forgetting past history, anti-Americanism became transformed into support for the Taliban in their fight against the US. Over a period of time anti-Americanism became synonymous with the resistance being put up by the Taliban. For a few weeks the harsh edicts of the Taliban were forgotten in Muslim societies and their new role as doughty warriors against American imperialism became their public face. The Taliban had won a great psychological victory. It helped boost their morale and allowed them to augment their manpower resources from the inexhaustible reservoir in Pakistan. Had the war in Afghanistan dragged on for a longer period it would not have come as a surprise to see more Pakistanis than Afghans fighting in Afghanistan against the Northern Alliance forces or the US led intervention forces. The unexpectedly swift withdrawal from Kabul in disarray and subsequent rout of the Taliban changed the equation.

Personalities have, more often than not, played a dominant role in warfare. This has been equally pronounced in the present struggle in Afghanistan. It required the mystique of the unlettered Taliban supreme leader and the sophisticated bin Laden to collect together a terror machine capable of hitting the US in its solar plexus in continental USA, the first time in nearly 200 years, and retaining, thereafter, the ability to threaten Americans and their assets practically everywhere in the world. Sadly for the US public the realization that it was the USA itself that, with the help of Pakistan, created these monsters can hardly ameliorate the suffering. Speculation will be rife as to the intimacy of those links in the intelligence, business and other spheres that may never come to light. People like bin Laden have an inbuilt advantage in perpetuating their mystique. To begin with the new recruits for *jehad* against the US being trained in thousands of *madrasas* in Pakistan, where they continue to be safe from US bombing, are taught from an early age to revere the Taliban supremo and bin Laden as saviours of Islam. For the rest of the Arab world, and Muslim societies elsewhere, irrespective of whether their brand of Islam is subscribed to or not, bin Laden becomes a cult figure by the sheer audacity of the attacks attributed to him by the

US. The pattern of the initial US response elevated bin Laden to a stature at par with that of the US president. At a later stage he surpassed it. For the first time after Nasser of Egypt a figure had arisen with the ability to enthuse the entire Arab world and much of the Muslim world.

It was a delicate issue that could not be perceived as clearly in the USA as would be possible for people who were not directly involved. It happened because the government of the United States, at its highest reaches, remained unaware of the effect of their public pronouncements in the minds of large swathes of the global public exposed to the Anglo-American media channels and the channels in their own countries that reported such pronouncements. After the initial phase of presidential speeches for uniting the US public and for orchestrating a global response to the scourge of terrorism, the President of the USA made direct appeals to Osama bin Laden or the Taliban supremo, as if they were heads of respected nations at par with China or Russia. The same applied to the ultimatums issued to them. It was not a personal confrontation between President Bush and Osama bin Laden. The mistake was made in the past when President Bush senior in an earlier era allowed the confrontation between USA and Iraq to become a direct confrontation between the US President and President Saddam Hussain of Iraq. To that extent, it would have served US policy goals better if ultimatums to the heads of Al Qaeda or the Taliban had been made at levels lower than the US President.

The other important leader on the Afghan scene who, in his own way, could have matched the charisma of Omar or bin Laden was Ahmed Shah Masood. His assassination could have a major effect on the future of Afghanistan. The Lion of Panjshir embodied in his person qualities that could have propelled him to the top of any future dispensation in Afghanistan. That a coalition as disparate as the Northern Alliance acknowledged – albeit grudgingly - his military prowess and sagacity as a leader, speaks volumes for General Masood.

8

Analysing the Military Strategy of the Intervention Forces

The US was comprehensively surprised by the WTC and Pentagon attacks on September 11, 2001. The sheer scale and audacity was breathtaking. It winded the top US hierarchy for a full twenty-four hours before the decision-making apparatus became demonstrably in some form of control. One of the greatest assets of the perpetrators was the surprise factor. It was total. It was akin to Pearl Harbour, perhaps, more so. There was no entity in the USA – at the federal or state level – that had any idea as to what was happening. The thought is frightening. Had the Cold War not been over and had there been a state of hostility, or near hostility, between the USA and any of the non-Western nuclear powers it is not inconceivable that a nuclear exchange may have ensued. Suppose the attack on the Pentagon had coincided with the previous year's stand off with China. What is even more frightening is that after the traumatic incident a global conclave to urgently go into the matter did not take place at the highest priority. It may never take place till a still bigger tragedy overtakes the world. In just a few mesmerizing days after the tragedy the nations of the world turned their back on the *greater tragedy* that could have ensued and commenced a new round of jockeying for influence in the Great Game in Central Asia.

Since surprise and audacity were the hallmark of the September 11 attacks the question must be posed, in the

USA, in the UN and the world at large, as to why there was such an abysmal intelligence failure on the part of all the agencies concerned with national security in the USA and the Western world. No matter what was put out through the official releases it is unbelievable that sufficient inputs were not available in USA and Pakistan to anticipate and ward off the attacks. Leaving Pakistan aside for the time being (see page 203) the conclusion becomes inescapable that early signs that something was afoot - though not its nature - were deliberately suppressed and ignored as part of an establishment consensus on the subject. Horrifying as it may sound, such things have happened before – in USA and other countries.

There are two main reasons for it. The first was that the people required to make such assessments never for a moment dreamed that something major was afoot. They surmised that terrorist attacks of the type that had taken place earlier would not be repeated in the USA. That they could be carried out in the USA and could be of an order or several orders of magnitude higher did not cross anybody's mind because – again perhaps rightly – it was felt that no nation or organization could be mad enough to hit the USA in a manner that would invite certain and massive retaliation - retaliation that would write 'finis' to the tale of the perpetrators. It might still happen.

The second and more important reason was the fact that the military industrial complex was hell bent on going ahead with the National Missile Defence (NMD) system, regardless of opposition, regardless of all else. Billions of dollars were in the pipeline for the initial phase of NMD. Under no circumstances could these outlays be jeopardized. Had the warning bells being sounded about the efficacy of low cost threats, or asymmetric threats, been allowed to become shriller, it would have led to Congressional committees and the Senate questioning the outlays *de novo*. Unfortunately ,for USA - and the world - no meaningful investigations into the lapse would be allowed to take place. Like the fire in the Pakistan General Headquarters that destroyed the records of Pakistan military's support to bin Laden and Al Qaeda, similar document losses would be arranged in the headquarters of the concerned agencies; in a far more sophisticated manner, of course.

The WTC and Pentagon attacks achieved total surprise; followed by days of consternation and sympathetic detonation of the myth of invincibility. It took a while for the US to recover its composure at the level of the national executive. It may take much longer for US society to recover its equilibrium. Internal assessments carried out post-September 11 would have revealed that terrorism emanating from the Pakistan–Afghanistan hinterland would continue to have the ability to menace the Western world, primarily the USA and its assets, almost anywhere in the world, until the time that the *jehadi* menace was extirpated at its source.

What followed was a military deployment to create the base for further military operations in the region. Whether these were to be of short-term or long duration would be contingent upon several factors whose locus was in and around the Taliban held territory in Afghanistan. The most important factors would be: the degree of support available from the Pakistan military government; Taliban's ability to withstand the aerial onslaughts; attitude of Russia and Iran; availability of bases in Central Asia; the attitude and capability of the Northern Alliance; intelligence inputs; efficacy of interdiction of the Taliban achieved in Afghanistan; degree of unrest in the Muslim world; degree of tacit support from Muslim rulers traditionally allied to the USA; attitude of China and other regional players; cohesiveness of the Western alliance to withstand the strains of prolonged military operations in the face of anti-war demonstrations that would surely follow; follow up terrorist activity and the like. The behaviour of oil prices, global economic recession and factors allied to global trade would be aspects that the US establishment would have looked at, though not in very great detail, before undertaking retaliatory actions. After a long period of anti-UN rhetoric the US government and the legislators in Washington suddenly discovered the virtues of a United Nations that they themselves had rendered largely ineffective after the end of the Cold War.

The dilemma faced by the US president would have been very real in those fateful days before embarking upon a course of action that had a built in element of irreversibility about it. This was the decision to intervene militarily in Afghanistan in order to flush out Osama bin Laden. Flushing out Osama bin Laden would entail the destruction of the Taliban. At a later stage it would entail the destruction of the factories and the systems that mass produce the committed manpower that constitute the Taliban's inexhaustible supply of the faithful who could be trained for suicide missions anywhere in the world. There would have been several pathways for achieving the US aim. Probably, it was the clamour for retaliation that had been built up in the USA that would have impelled the US president toward the direction that he took. Conceivably it would have squared up with his instincts, in this regard. These were revealed to the world by the pattern of his immediate responses. Whether they were right or wrong should be left to posterity. While the media - and countries not directly affected by the tragic happenings - may sit in judgment, it has to be remembered that many, if not most, human beings and many of the leaders would have, in all probability, expressed similar sentiments in their unguarded moments as a first response to the enormous tragedy that befell the US. President George W. Bush of USA was no exception. He was a politician, like other ordinary politicians around the world. He was propelled by circumstances and money power to the US presidency. Most of the world leaders of today were ordinary politicians who grew into their jobs as leaders of their countries. Barring a few exceptions none of them had, or has, the charisma, wisdom or the other attributes that go to make a great leader. Shorn off their high office they descend fast into the realm of the commonplace.

A discussion along these lines becomes necessary because of the invasiveness and pervasiveness of round the clock media activity. It prevents decision-makers from sitting back and reflecting deeply on their response patterns to national calamities before making their views known to the public. The initial response, which can very often differ from the measured response after additional inputs and advice are available, gets foisted upon the incumbent and limits the persons room for manoeuver once it has been broadcast around the world. At its worst, it sets in motion certain responses on the part of the adversary who could easily mistake the initial response reported in the media as the probable course of action likely to be adopted. Hence, a negative spiral that could have been avoided had instant media exposure in the immature reflexive state not taken place comes into being. Whether the blame for this lies at the door of the media networks or on the compulsive need of political leaders to seek and use the media – media manipulation – is a question that cannot be easily answered. By its very nature, it varies from country to country and from person to person. Whatever be its nature, it becomes part of the war fighting strategy of the adversaries and their backers. Disinformation and misinformation, allied to media distortions, deliberate or unintended, have become an important aspect of the strategy of warfare in the 21st century.

The second major dilemma faced by the US establishment, in view of the gravity of the provocation, was the need to send a message to all future adversaries of the USA. It was as much a need for reassuring the US public. The message had to make clear that a physical assault on the USA could not possibly go unpunished. Were the punishment not to be of a severity that was merited when an attack of this type is carried out on US territory, it would have been mistaken as a sign of weakness and could encourage future would be attackers. Additionally, it was not an isolated case, in spite of the severity of the attack and the quantum of damage inflicted. It was the culmination of a series of attacks against US troops, embassies and a US warship. The damage inflicted in the September 11 attacks, whether calculated or otherwise, was at several levels. At the first level, it was the *symbolism* of the targets chosen, their physical destruction, and the number of deaths resulting from the attacks. At the second level the damage was to the American economy. The ramification of the economic damage could go well beyond the damage to the aviation and insurance sectors. At the third level the damage was to the US defensive posture perfected since the end of the Cold War. In the build up to NMD and space warfare these attacks turned US conventional military wisdom, based on the Revolution in Military Affairs, on its head. It would take a while to readjust to the new patterns of threat – to the US, to US military deployments, to US citizens and US assets worldwide. The fourth level of damage inflicted was the exploding of the myth of US invincibility. It demonstrated that when hit hard, and unexpectedly, the US establishment and public were capable of floundering as helplessly as the rest of the global community when exposed to such unexpected blows. It showed that human beings are the same everywhere. Terror hurts; in the rest of the world *and* in USA. The distinction that had become blurred for the USA over several decades was removed. The damage at the fifth level, arguably the most important level, was the blow given to the collective US psyche. It brought in fear. Stark fear. It was of a nature to which audiences were exposed only in movies. Hereafter, fear would stalk US citizens even in the USA, their safe haven that was no longer so safe, and when moving out of the country.

Hence, while the ground situation in Afghanistan may prove more or less difficult than the US government imagined, its dilemma remains. The fear that has permeated the US public will not go away till the time that US citizens everywhere are convinced that the people who launched the September 11 attacks have been dealt with effectively. While stray incidents of terror could always take place, organized terror of the type emanating from the Pakistan-Afghanistan region represents a level of threat never experienced ever before by US society, not even at the height of the Cold War. Nor even during the two World Wars. During the Vietnam War and other US involvements in military operations, continental USA was considered to be relatively safe. The other aspect which impels the US toward strong military action is the fact that the Taliban and Osama bin Laden, backed by their supporters in many countries, not only declared war on the USA, they declared *open season on all Americans*. These were reinforced through televised messages broadcast repeatedly. Therefore, whatever critics of US policy, anti-war demonstrators and pacifist worldwide may have to say in regard to US policy, they will not count for much in US decision-making unless they are able to demonstrate that the threat to USA and its citizens no longer exists. Or, if it exists it is no longer at a level that US citizens need to lose sleep over. Hence, whatever the tenor of the debate that rages in this regard, the US option whether to wage war or not, did not really exist. War was declared on the USA. USA had to fight back. From a realistic standpoint, therefore, the debate that can take place on this issue is limited only to whether, under the circumstances, the USA could have used different military strategies to achieve its stated goals. More than its security, the credibility of the USA as a superpower was at stake the moment it decided to intervene militarily in Afghanistan. Whatever it took, the US had gone in to win. It could not afford a second Vietnam. A second Vietnam would spell the demise of USA as the remaining superpower. Within a matter of weeks and months the stakes for both sides had become exorbitantly high.

Once the chips were down and the die was cast, it became possible to re-evaluate the US military strategy. Since it could be many years before those outside the limited decision-making circle around the US president would become privy to the various options that might have been discussed and discarded prior to exercising the military option and the operational strategy decided upon to prosecute that option, the take-off point for the analysis that follows has perforce to be the deployment pattern on the ground in and around Afghanistan and the manner in which the military retaliation was commenced as a war fighting strategy. Since the deployment of US forces was openly effected – not that it could have been concealed – it became apparent that the US led forces had been able to create air bases in the north (Uzbekistan) and to the east and south (four known bases in Pakistan) close to the border with Afghanistan. In addition, it secured over-flight rights from some of the other neighbouring countries, in case of dire need or for casualty evacuation. A formidable naval presence was also established in the Arabian Sea so that carrier based operations could be carried out. The military war in Afghanistan was prosecuted under the aegis of US Central Command. Intelligence sharing was tied up with all the neighbourhood countries, most importantly with Pakistan, Russia, India, Saudi Arabia and a few other countries. From the beginning the US establishment would not have been unmindful of the fact that intelligence sharing with Pakistan was a double-edged sword. In all probability this double-edged sword would be sharper towards the American side. Real time inputs to the Taliban would be available at all levels. Seeing the degree of intimacy that had existed between the Pakistan establishment and the Taliban the inputs made available to the Taliban could be acted upon immediately, without re-verification. On the US side the element of doubt would always remain.

During the period of the open deployment of US forces around Afghanistan the Taliban had sufficient time to accurately assess the likely pattern of US military operations inside Afghanistan once the deployment had been completed. Whatever the gaps in their knowledge, these were filled up by inputs from the Pakistan military, the ISI and sympathizers in Pakistan. Tactical readjustments could have been carried out accordingly. Therefore, the element of surprise that can often be a war-winning factor was almost totally absent when the air strikes commenced on October 7, 2001. The Taliban had had sufficient warning to enable them to hunker down. While many critics would be found for the US policy of putting almost all their eggs in the Pakistan military basket at the commencement of hostilities, the US government may have felt that it did not have much of a choice in the matter.

The question uppermost in the minds of many people would be as to whether the US could have done without the support of the head of the Pakistan state. Clearly it could not have. Irrespective of the double game that both sides – the US and Pakistan military – would be playing and would continue to play to the end, they had no option other than picking up the threads of their earlier engagement during the Zia-ul-Haq era. While the Pakistan government had committed itself to supporting the US military action from the soil of Pakistan, it had to be seen to be prevaricating for the benefit of its own population in order to contain the unrest that would ensue. It might have been apparent to the Pakistan military establishment that both sides could benefit from a clear victory of the US in Afghanistan. For the US the destruction of the Taliban and its replacement by a government in Kabul acceptable to them would represent a major victory. Added to the capture of Osama bin Laden and the neutralization of Al Qaeda in Afghanistan it would have met almost all the short-term military objectives of the USA. For the Pakistan military a government favourable to Pakistan would be the outcome most desired. However, Pakistan could settle for a government in Kabul that was not hostile to Pakistan and not overly friendly with any of the other countries in the region. Furthermore, the comprehensive defeat of the Taliban in Afghanistan would automatically degrade the threat posed by the burgeoning *talibanisation* of Pakistan society. The military government would then be in a position to deal with the reduced level of threat from Islamic fundamentalism, followed by a programme of modernization of education and de-*jehadisation* of the *madrasas*. At that stage there could be a genuine convergence between the long-term interests of USA and Pakistan. This could be the ideal outcome that could lead to the economic rehabilitation of Pakistan and phased programme for restoration of democracy. Whether such an ideal outcome could be brought about would depend more on the earnestness of the Pakistan military to support US operations in Afghanistan. A dedicated commitment on the part of the Pakistan military establishment would enhance the likelihood of successful US operations manifold. Any foot dragging by the Pakistan military establishment would, of necessity, increase the likelihood of prolonged high-tech warfare for the USA, which, in turn, would increase the collateral damage to civilians and the flow of refugees to Pakistan. The possibility that the Pakistan military deliberately orchestrated this outcome by luring the USA into this trap cannot be entirely ruled out. Opprobrium in the Muslim world due to prolonged bombing would force the US establishment to increase its dependence on the Pakistan military. The choice before the Pakistan military government was crystal clear. Either they supported the US effort whole-heartedly and brought about the transformation of Pakistan or they hedged their bets. The worst-case scenario for Pakistan would have been to fall between the two stools.

The US had several options open to it *before* committing its forces in Afghanistan. Once committed into fighting the Taliban militarily, there were again a number of options available at the *outset* to progress the operations. Whether the operational strategy implemented on the ground to deal with the Taliban and Osama bin Laden was the best option available only time will tell. Needless to say, that once a particular option is put into effect the other options stand discarded or degraded as time goes by. After the launch of military operations there can be no such thing as *status quo ante*, in its literal sense. Any return to an earlier state has to factor in the events that intervened and their consequences. Unfortunately for America the military options exercised at the beginning became hostage to political considerations. In the realm of political considerations, while several factors - and neighbouring countries - came into play, the immediate trade off related mainly to weighing up the inter se distribution of effort between coordination with Pakistan, backing of the Northern Alliance, coordination with Russia and to an extent the coordination with Iran and Uzbekistan. In its efforts to balance the conflicting requirements of these countries the US may have ended up by dissipating some of its military effort and not gaining a decisive edge on the ground in any of the sectors in the first few weeks when it had the initiative to progress operations in any manner deemed fit.

To a large extent, early military success was (allowed to be) compromised by the long-term, post-intervention strategies of the USA. It was compromised also due to the conflicting pulls of the coalition partners gathered in the region to support US operations. These shifted the focus away from the immediate operational imperative. Such shifting away of focus from the main point of decisive impact can fatally flaw a military operation. Whether it introduced a fatal flaw in the immediate military intervention strategy of the USA in Afghanistan cannot be answered with any degree of certainty. Mid-term corrections could always be applied. Here again, whether the US would have been in a position to apply them without offending one or more of the coalition partners remains a moot question. For the USA, consideration of its long-term geopolitical interest meant ensuring the stability of the pro-American military regime in Pakistan. From available indications an Anglo-American military presence in Central Asia, Afghanistan and Pakistan on a semi-permanent basis appears to be on the cards. The US long-term presence has implications for China, Russia, Iran and India besides Pakistan and Afghanistan themselves. While perceptions of the concerned countries mentioned above would differ an aspect to be considered would be whether US military presence in the region would help or exacerbate regional stability, both in the short-term as well as the long-term.

A strategy that the US could have adopted in the initial period would have been massive logistics and close air support to the Northern Alliance to allow for the capture of certain key towns in northern, central and western Afghanistan. These would have automatically reduced the area of influence under the Taliban. As a spin off, besides the destruction of the Taliban forces involved in defending the towns against Northern Alliance assaults, the area available to Osama bin Laden to hide would also have been considerably reduced, that is in case bin Laden had not already escaped to another country. To alleviate somewhat the fears of the other coalition partners, mainly Pakistan, the US could have laid down a forward limit for Northern Alliance ingress into central and western Afghanistan. This limit could have been decided upon jointly between USA and Russia as guarantors for the Northern Alliance respecting the laid down limit. Had this strategy been pursued with vigour the US forces would have been able to establish sizeable operational bases within Afghanistan. It would have allowed them to divide, isolate and interdict the remainder Taliban elements and defeat them in detail, in a pattern decided by the US commanders. Under these circumstances the initiative would have remained with the US forces and the Taliban forces could have been kept off balance all the time.

In their desire to retain maximum advantage for themselves and not afford too much leeway to the regional alliance partners, the US kept sending conflicting signals to the different supporting partners active on the ground. That the Pakistan military establishment had to be coerced into giving support meant that they could not be fully trusted with all the details of the strategy being followed by the Americans. While this holding back could have been a measure of abundant caution it also ended up by confusing the Pakistan military supporters; the confusion was further compounded by the number of high-level Western visitors to Islamabad. Although these visitors were clear about their agenda, they did not speak the same language as regard to the advice given to the Pakistan head of state. There was a subtle shift of emphasis in each case, reflecting the bias and prejudices of their respective governments or departments. The confusion was also added to by the differing perceptions, as conveyed to the Pakistan military authorities, by the representatives of the US departments of state, defence and the US Central Command. As if all this were not enough, the US president took it upon himself to publicly chide the Pakistan president on television about the statements made by the latter on the manner in which the war in Afghanistan was being progressed. Seeing that he was the most important local supporter of US operations in Afghanistan, it denied room for manoeuver to the Pakistan president to manage his flock. These rebuttals emanating from Washington were unnecessary and served only to compromise the position of the president of Pakistan, who was already doing a precarious tightrope act.

In like manner conflicting signals were given to the Northern Alliance. At the beginning it appeared that the Americans were pinning their hopes on them. However, the result of the lack of coordination or misinterpreted signals soon began to show. The premature, half-hearted and uncoordinated attack on the outskirts of Mazar -I Sharif not long after the commencement of hostilities was a case in point. In the eventuality the Northern Alliance forces were pushed back several tens of kilometers by the fierce Taliban reaction. Within the Northern Alliance, instead of strengthening the disparate factions, the Americans gave the impression of making separate deals with some of the Alliance partners, most notably the Uzbek warlord. Logistic and close air support was also not forthcoming in the earlier stages before the Taliban had consolidated. The Northern Alliance commanders kept chafing about the uncertain conditions under which they were operating.

Perhaps the most important lesson to emerge from the military operations in Afghanistan is the need for the US military establishment to review its war fighting strategy for different theatres around the world. The success attributed to missiles and aerial bombardment in bringing the Gulf War to a successful conclusion without heavy and prolonged ground fighting had a profound influence on US military doctrine for the ensuing decades. Instead of a corrective being applied to the value of coordinated ground and air actions to bring them to a center point of operational equilibrium the pendulum was allowed to swing to the other extreme. It was reinforced by the Revolution in Military Affairs. Whatever the misgivings that remained, these were submerged by the capitulation achieved in Yugoslavia over the Kosovo affair due to prolonged missile and aircraft bombings.

While on the subject of the operations in Afghanistan, it is possible that the US military establishment might have gone overboard on the use of high-tech weapons. In the process, elementary soldiering skills perfected since ages might be atrophying. There is a whole range of viable low-tech options for flushing out adversaries that does not seem to have been examined by the US forces. Although the old pattern again proved successful in Afghanistan due to the unexpected decision of the Taliban to give up Kabul without fight there can be situations where over-reliance on high-tech could prove counter productive.

Since the military intervention in Afghanistan was undertaken as part of the global fight against terrorism, it signified the US resolve to take the fight to the very heart of terrorism, the Afghanistan-Pakistan region. Even if the US had achieved early success in ousting the Taliban and neutralising Al Qaeda, which it apparently did not, the fact remains that the wellsprings of terrorism have got embedded so deeply in the *madrasa* culture that it has become a self-replenishing fount. Its elimination will take much more than military success in Afghanistan. Realising this fact, the US government had declared that the global fight against terrorism had many components. The magnitude of the threat entailed global cooperation on a scale seldom attempted before in the quasi-military sphere. In the aftermath of the twin towers attack, when the scale of the tragedy began to sink into the global consciousness after viewing the unnerving TV images of the trauma as it unfolded, the heart of the civilized world went out spontaneously to the American people in their hour of grief. The cobbling together of a global coalition and the Security Council resolution on terrorism were instinctive responses of the global community shrinking before the horror of the new menace appearing on its horizon. The US government could have capitalized on this support to effectively eliminate the threat posed to civilised society by mindless terror visited upon innocent civilians. The US government began well. Somewhere along the way it might have allowed a historic opportunity to slip by.

How did this happen? It happened because the instinct of the cold warrior so firmly imprinted in the US military establishment could not remain suppressed for long. It was not long before the cold warriors took over.

Instead of concentrating their energies on fighting global terror, the US military establishment sensed an un-hoped for opportunity to extend its military reach into Central Asia. Alongside, the military-industrial complex saw an opportunity for increased military expenditure and for the testing of more lethal weapons on the devastated Afghanistan countryside, the perfect testing site for deep penetration weapons. There would be no limits imposed on the testing. At this point the discomfiture of the two countries without whose support global terror could not be effectively dealt with, Russia and China increased. They communicated their disquiet to the USA. Discerning the shift in US geopolitical strategy the global coalition began to show the first sign of cracks. It would only be a matter of time before the US oil lobby took over the lead role in the fight against global terrorism. At that point Iran could also opt out. It is still not too late for the US establishment to veer back towards global harmonization for tackling the shadowy adversaries before bigger tragedies befall the US and other innocent people around the world. At the very least, the USA will have to realign its strategy to accommodate the minimum Russian concern in Central Asia and Afghanistan. Iran will automatically stand reassured. The USA could still get bogged down in Afghanistan. If it does, it will not be on account of a deteriorating military situation. In all probability, it would be on account of its inability to distinguish between the contrary pulls of the Great Game and the Great Terror that it set out to fight.

A military strategy that could have led to a favourable outcome for the intervention forces, without resorting in the early stages to the type of aerial bombing that ended up by building support for the Taliban, had been clearly outlined in the talk on 'Dealing with the Afghanistan-Pakistan Cauldron: The Global Perspective' delivered in August 2000. It has been reproduced at the end of the book under the rubric, 'Epilogue as Prologue'.

9

Random Press Samplings (Pakistan)

Excerpts taken at random from Pakistan publications of the period leading up to September 11, 2001.

- *Report in The News International,* May 10, 2001.
- "THE LOGICAL objective of the *jihad* against India is the destruction of the US". Urdu daily *Ausaf* quoted in *The Friday Times,* January 29, 2001.
- "If US attacks Afghanistan, then we would start massacre of Americans. US is a global terrorist and wherever suppression is being committed in the world, behind that the US hand is definite". Maulana Abdul Gaffur, Central Secretary General of Jamiat-Ulema-Islam(F), quoted in Urdu daily *Khabrain,* October 31, 2000.

"We will turn the US into hell if any damage is done to Osama", *Ausaf,* October 25, 2000, quoting Jamiat-Ulema-Islam statement at a conference held in Rawalpindi on October 24, 2000.

"Clinton and Vajpayee are the biggest terrorists", Lashkar-e-Toyba chief, addressing a meeting at Gandiyal, Punjab, on November 4, 2000 quoted in *Khabrain,* November 5, 2000.

"Attacks by *fedayeen* (suicide squads) have shaken the power corridors in Washington and made Vajpayee feel jittery". *Ausaf,* December 31, 2000.

- "Delhi, Calcutta, Mumbai and Washington are the real targets of the militants. Muslims should cooperate with militants for dominance of Islam in the world", Harkat-ul-Mujahideen chief, Maulana Fazlur Rahman Khalil's statement in Islamabad, quoted in *Ausaf,* December 27, 2000.

- "If the US dared to attack Afghanistan and Osama, we will teach them a lesson and will turn Afghanistan into a graveyard of the US forces, the US attack on Afghanistan will be considered an attack on Islam and a befitting reply will be given to the European world and to the US also", from a joint statement issued by Students of Pakistani Madrassahs at a meeting in Islamabad on October 20, 2000, quoted in *Khabrain,* October 21, 2000.

- "Sipah-e-Sahaba announced that one lakh militants will be sent to Israel. It demanded that Gen. Pervez Musharraf launch *jihad* against India and Israel immediately", Maulana Ziaul Qasmi at a press conference, quoted in *The Nation,* October 26, 2000.

- "A billion and thirty crore Muslims of the world should wage *jihad* against Israel, India, the US and Russia. They will be no more and only Islam will rule all over the world", Al Badr militants quoted in *Nawa-I-Waqt"* November 21, 2000.

- "*Jehad* has become the foremost duty of the Muslim community against Israel, the US and India. They don't understand the language of talks. They only understand the language of sword". Bakht Zameen, Amir, Al-Badr, at a press conference at Mardan, North West Frontier Province, on October 25, 2000, quoted in *Khabrain,* October 26, 2000.

10

Epilogue as Prologue

(The talk reproduced in the Epilogue was delivered thirteen months prior to the events of September 11, 2001)

Dealing with the Afghan-Pak Cauldron: The Global Perspective

*(Talk delivered by **Maj. Gen. Vinod Saighal** at the United Service Institution of India on August 9, 2000)*

The Cauldron Simmers

The 'Afghanistan-Pakistan Cauldron' (hereafter referred to as the A-P Cauldron, or more aptly just the Cauldron), indicates a region in turmoil. Afghanistan and Pakistan are not only in a state of ferment themselves; the spillover from the Cauldron is causing concern in many parts of the world. Here is what the Chief Executive of Pakistan himself has to say on the subject. In an interview given in Rawalpindi to AP nearly a month ago he reportedly said:

> "Pakistan is one of the most difficult countries in the world to govern, smack in the middle of the most dangerous region in the world"

Exactly half a century earlier Owen Latimore described the region as:

> "A whirlpool in which meet political currents flowing from China, Russia, India and the Moslem Middle East."
>
> -Owen Latimore, 'Eurasia, the World's New Centre of Gravity'.

A true enough description, but in 1950 the author could not have foreseen the disintegration of the powerful Soviet empire or, for that matter, the suddenness of its demise. The genesis of the post-World War II Afghan tragedy can be traced back to the competition for influence between many countries after the retreat of

Great Britain as a world power. This study of the current situation confines itself to the vacuum resulting from the sudden collapse of USSR. With its dissolution at the end of 1991 a new era of global geopolitics commenced whose effects were most pronounced in the A-P cauldron.

The mobilisation of religious orthodoxy for giving battle to an entrenched ideology (communism), in a country under occupation (Afghanistan), makes an interesting case study in itself. Of greater interest at the present time is the study of the chilling transformation that was engineered in the purely 'defensive' mobilisation of the religious orthodoxy (for vacating aggression) to one of 'offensive' religious fundamentalism with pan-Islamic overtones, capable of conducting terrorism on a global scale. Religious mobilisation by itself, however, could not have succeeded in repelling aggression without massive military and financial assistance.

Circumstances have since changed. Global alignments have changed. Foes have turned into friends. The Cauldron continues to simmer. Causing untold suffering to neighbours; no less to its own people. The sequence of countries mentioned in the title, Afghanistan-Pakistan, was not intended to follow the alphabetical progression from A to P. It is indicative of a grand reversal that could be taking place, might indeed have already taken place. It is no longer Afghanistan that provides the supposed strategic depth to Pakistan. It is Pakistan that now provides strategic back up to the Taliban. It is a fatal embrace. Neither party can disengage unilaterally without delivering a body blow to the 'other'. The other, in the case of Pakistan, does not represent the state of Pakistan. It refers exclusively to the military - religious fundamentalist combine that seeks to perpetuate its hold on the state machinery through terror, or the potential for letting loose terror, or the threat of waging nuclear war.

Axially (the A-P axis), and internally in Pakistan, the tail has started wagging the dog. In the first case the Taliban factor impinges heavily on state policy and in the latter case the *jehadis* dictate terms to the Pak military. It is essential for the world to appreciate this point. Because when one talks of a nuclear Pakistan what is being talked about, in reality, is not the state of Pakistan but the combine that appears to be all-powerful in the Afghan-Pak cauldron. Doubtless, the combine has suffered recent setbacks due to international pressure, prolonged drought in Afghanistan and the precarious economic situation of Pakistan. The impression is gaining ground that the combined effect of the setbacks might have enfeebled the regimes in power. The world would be playing into their hands should it mistake the tactical surface re-adjustments being carried out as a change of heart. In many respects, hidden from the public gaze, this combine is going from strength to strength. The logic becomes irrefutable. The Pakistan military controls the nuclear arsenal of Pakistan. The Pakistan military is increasingly coming under the sway of the fundamentalists in Pakistan. The coupling of the military and the fundamentalists had spawned the Taliban. The offspring is now a potent voice in the triad. Therefore, going purely by present trends, if not immediately, certainly a few years down the road, the nuclear arsenal of Pakistan will be in the hands of this not so holy triad.

Currently, each of the elements forming the triad finds themselves in a bind. The euphoria that the Taliban initially generated on first taking over has dissipated. They have been successful mainly in alienating their neighbours. Internally there is simmering discontent. On the other side the Pakistani generals who run the country are in a similar situation. They were directly responsible for the Kargil debacle. Their gamble failed. Gamblers - especially, military leaders - who lose are expected to pay the price. In this case they carried out a coup against the civilian government and made the erstwhile Prime Minister pay the price. They are thus left with no option but to continue with cross border terrorism in the desperate hope that the world will take note. There is nothing else that they can show for their misadventure.

The women of Afghanistan who suffered the most in the war-ravaged countryside are being brutally crushed as never before. It may not be long before the same treatment is extended to the liberated segments of Pakistan society. A far cry from the dream of Pakistan's founding father. It has taken the military and the mullahs just fifty years to turn his legacy on its head. Here is what Mr. Jinnah had to say on the status of women:

> *"No nation can rise to the height of glory unless your women are side by side with you; we are victims of evil customs. It is a crime against humanity that our women are shut up within the four walls of the houses as prisoners. There is no sanction anywhere for the deplorable condition in which our women have to live."*
>
> -Pakistan's founding father, Mohammad Ali Jinnah, in a speech in 1944.

As reported in the press (*The Statesman*, July 30, 2000) the recent arrest and imprisonment of an American grandmother - Mary MacMakin, 72, who spent 24 years as an aid worker and set up the Physiotherapy and Rehabilitation Support for Afghanistan (PARSA) in 1996 - signaled the start of a new wave of repression by the Islamic regime. She blames the development on the Taliban's heavy casualties in its annual summer offensive in the north. "Its put them in a bad mood and they are taking it out on women".

Taking it out on women' seems to be a common feature of the military and the mullahs. The Pakistani army perfected the technique in Bangladesh when they felt that things might turn out badly for them. They raped or killed a hundred thousand women. May be more. Not to be outdone the Taliban have gone a step further. They have set up the Ministry for the Prevention of Vice and the Promotion of Virtue. The virtue emanating out of the A-P cauldron is palpable. It left a hundred pilgrims dead in a recent attack.

The silent majority of the people in Pakistan have been watching with dismay the gradual erosion of their liberties. The educated elite hope that world opinion will come to their rescue should things really get out of hand. These are vain hopes, of people unable to bestir themselves to oppose the creeping *talibanisation* overtaking their land. They too have had ample warning. Should they fail to mobilise themselves to defeat the *jehadis*, while they are able to, they might have to meet the fate of the women of Afghanistan. The monsters being nurtured for cross border terrorism could well turn upon them one fine day. It has happened before. It can happen again.

Who created this frightening scenario? At the beginning the United States and Saudi Arabia, to oppose Soviet domination. They were fighting their arch foe. They could not have known the outcome. Now the baton seems to have landed in the lap of China. It is fast becoming the most dominant player in the region. Having provided the Pakistan military with the wherewithal to wage nuclear war against India the Chinese have become the principal benefactors of Pakistan, and by extension, the Taliban as well. The Chinese have always been the superior strategists. They realise that by controlling the Pak military they, in fact, exercise or will soon exercise *de facto* control over the potential for global mischief that inheres in the A-P cauldron. That is not to say that the Chinese encourage, or would wish to encourage, terrorism emanating from the Cauldron. It is not inconceivable that China, at some stage might use its leverage to moderate the extremism in the region. Such speculation of a moderating influence will remain a big IF. It will depend to an extent on the policies pursued by the United States in setting up a national or theatre missile defence shield in violation of the 1972 ABM Treaty. The Chinese strategic vision has always been masterly.

Masterly or not, as in the earlier case, they too can never be sure of the outcome. Pakistan seems to have already taken the decision to trade in nuclear materials. In the not too distant future they will undercut China in the rates offered for missiles as well. The Chinese should take heed.

The Muslim fundamentalists are mass - producing canon fodder in the name of *jehad*. Actually the term 'jehad' is a misnomer. It is a convenient tool for acquiring political power through violence. Young boys, not even in their teens, usually the surplus fifth and sixth sons from large and poor families, seldom the first or second, are lured away to be indoctrinated into fanaticism and hatred. A throw back to the dark ages of every race and religion; perfect emulation of what happened in Nazi Germany and continues to happen where such elements are in the ascendant elsewhere in the world.

THE GLOBAL PERSPECTIVE

It would be facile for the world at large to dismiss the hydra headed monster being spawned in the A-P cauldron as a regional problem affecting India, the Central Asian

Republics, parts of Russia and some others. While it *is* a major problem for the neighbours the global dimension of the problem is equally important. The United States could conceivably reach accommodation with the A-P authorities were their *bete noire*, Osama bin Laden to be surrendered to them. Neither they, nor the American public, have yet realised that bin Laden is just the most public face of a deeper danger confronting them. In nearly ten thousand *madrasas* strewn across the Cauldron a few hundred thousand new bin Laden clones are well on their way to reaching productive maturity. Their testing grounds are USA and India. Even more than the Quranic verses what is dinned into their young minds is the fanatical utterance 'death to America and the *kafirs*' (in India).

The remainder world, currently uninvolved, can also not afford to push the issue under the carpet as a problem for the neighbours, Russia and USA. Several entry points have been established in Europe. New bridgeheads are coming up elsewhere. Terrorism of the new variety, not linked to any specific issue, but political power play under the guise of religious fundamentalism - essentially programmed hatred in young minds, snatched from the cradle - knows no boundaries. It will strike where the handlers unleash their indoctrinated minions, mass-produced in the same way as any assembly line product.

An even deadlier menace is emerging from the A-P cauldron, namely, criminals committed for heinous offences are being promised their freedom should they undertake killings across the border. Not infrequently their targets turn out to be defenseless women and children, victims of indiscriminate bombings in the market place. It calls for not only international condemnation in the strongest terms, but *suo motu* action by the International Criminal Court, Interpol and other concerned international agencies.

At the moment the activity is mostly directed against India and a few other countries where the *jehadis* are active. If it remains unchecked, it is only a matter of time before these criminals are let loose on civilised society anywhere. It needs to be understood that criminals who have committed heinous crimes generally have psychopathic tendencies. Letting loose such individuals amongst law-abiding citizens should be deemed a crime against humanity. The guilt for such crimes rests with heads of organisations that use them for such ends as well as the heads of the concerned governments. They are as guilty as the criminals committing the outrages. Their prosecution should be authorised by the concerned international courts and international warrants for their arrest issued accordingly. It is one thing if underground 'criminal' organisations indulge in such activities. It is an entirely different matter if 'states' permit them as state policy. Should the international community not address the issue urgently the world may well witness an increase of this phenomenon - worldwide.

Since the religious fundamentalist turmoil was fuelled in Pakistan consequent to Gen. Zia-ul-Haq's need to garner support for the military regime it is time to take another look at Pakistan in the new century, from a global perspective. Pakistan served the interests of the West during the Cold War. So did many other nations around the world. The Cold War ended in the last century. The geopolitical compulsions of the 21st century have changed considerably from the conditions obtaining in the post-World War II years. Today Pakistan has embarked on an enterprise whose global ramifications, if it remains unchecked, are far too serious to contemplate with equanimity. It is no longer playing regional politics. The military-mullah dispensation in that country is playing with fire.

While Kashmir continues to be a convenient *casus belli*, the religious significance is deeper, not only for India, but for the world as well. Fundamental Islam, except on the fringes, was not a natural modern era phenomenon on the subcontinent. It became a religious ploy that suited interested groups in Pakistan, a sure-fire remedy for keeping them in business. The difference being that the rabidity at the fringes could become the norm should the world not act decisively. The combine in power, with military support from China, could soon be in a position to raise the nuclear ante at the subcontinental or global levels.

The Kashmir Valley was not a territorial prize *per se*. For the first set of raiders in 1947 the real prize was loot and rape. For their successors the prize is the quality referred to as 'Kashmiriyat'. A unique blend of *sufi* mysticism, religious tolerance and a liberal, joyous outlook on life that would be anathema to religious fundamentalists anywhere. They cannot accept 'a heaven on earth' with gurgling springs, laughing belles, haunting melodies and *joie de vivre* that over the centuries symbolised the beautiful Vale of Kashmir. A religious harmony that was a living challenge to their fundamentalism. For the A-P fundamentalists it became their poisoned chalice. Were it to be allowed to continue to blossom, its heady fragrance of a tolerant, humanising creed would imperil their hold. The two are incompatible. Kashmiriyat had to be destroyed, whatever the cost. Kashmir is the red herring. Even there, demographic swamping in Pakistan occupied Kashmir and the so-called Northern Areas (Gilgit, Baltistan) directly administered from Islamabad has rendered the plebiscite clause of the ancient UN resolution inoperative. Not to mention the ethnic cleansing that has been engineered through terrorist acts across the border.

Today the might of USA is deployed worldwide to bring bin Laden to book. He can play hide and seek indefinitely in the mountain remoteness of Afghanistan. What will happen when the multiplying bin Laden type legions fan out across the globe, take their terrifying toll of the non-believers, and scurry back to their sanctuary, beyond the pale of national and international law enforcement? Technology does not suffice to deal with them in the rugged terrain that obtains. This is no longer a band of terrorists threatening the world order. It is the state itself, which is on the way to becoming the master terrorist of the globe. Soon, it will be able to nourish all fundamentalist groups from their *madrasas*. Links have already been established with other drug mafias. The question then arises:

> "Is the world seriously expecting India to countenance with equanimity the talibanisation of the Vale of Kashmir"!

Unless the A-P cauldron is dealt with firmly on a global basis it will not be long before the contagion spreads to other countries having sizeable Islamic populations. In this category must be included Malaysia, Indonesia, the Philippines, Bangladesh, Myanmar and many countries in Central Asia and the Middle East - areas that hold almost eighty percent of the global oil reserves. Looked at globally - de-linked from country-specific fixations like bin Laden, Chechnya, Xinjiang, Kashmir and the like - the problem assumes a different perspective.

It is because of the fillip being given by the fundamentalist cells implanted from the Cauldron on ethnic divides in other countries that the world is witnessing increasing ethnic cleansing in areas that were earlier relatively free from this scourge. In the process economic development suffers and backwardness and poverty are accentuated. Ethnic cleansing in Indonesia got out of hand after the economic collapse of Indonesia; and because of the heightened insecurity caused by the daily killings nobody would like to invest in those areas. Perpetuating the vicious cycle of violence and poverty. Terrorism is considered by some to be the most flagrant form of defiance of the rule of law. How right! In areas where the militants and the military rule, law courts are replaced by kangaroo courts.

The Predicament of the Non-Militant Pakistanis

Historians writing about the French Revolution make the point that the disoriented people of France - nearly 27 million of them - allowed Robespierre and his small band of followers to actually coerce them through terror into accepting his dictatorship. What followed is well known. Over a quarter million people were sent to jail and about forty thousand guillotined after mock trials. When the people finally mustered the will to stand up it was found that at the outset the hard core had consisted of just a handful of people, precisely twenty-two. The people of Pakistan and, for that matter, law abiding citizens everywhere who see a gradual erosion of their freedoms under *jehad* type dispensations must realise that they alone are the guardians of their liberty. If they do not organise themselves to resist terror when it 'first' starts manifesting itself they too could go under one day.

The military and the mullahs are exporting *jehad* in the name of religion. It is ironic. As state policy, it is not being exported from any of the Arab countries that were the fountainhead of Islam. Genetically the vast majority of the Muslims in Pakistan are converts from the older religions of India. So, is it the ardour of the converted, needing to proclaim their *bona fides* from the rooftops, which one is witnessing? The behaviour is bizarre to say the least. Not many in the Arab world, to which they take a bow, seem to be clapping. In fact there are not many places left in the world, besides India, where the ordinary Pakistani is welcome. Who is to blame for this state of affairs? The military, the mullahs or the average Pakistani citizen for not standing up! Unless the people of Pakistan themselves decide to throw off their yoke the world could well decide to leave them to their fate.

The diplomatic isolation, which is a recent phenomenon, could become a permanent fixture should the military-mullah combine continue to brandish its newfound nuclear might. It is not adding to their stature. Only making the world aware of the need for concerted global action. Even the Chinese who supplied them the wherewithal should be having second thoughts.

Global Action to Deal with the Menace

The question then arises, "how does the world deal with this growing global menace emanating from the Cauldron"? Regional initiatives are obviously an important factor. Easier said than done. Geopolitical imbalances make neighbours in regions where stability has yet to be achieved suspicious of each other's motives. This is true in most parts of Asia and Africa. Whatever the state or nature of regional dissonance there are troublesome aspects, discussed earlier, which need remedial action at the global level. The foremost among these is the status of women. Does the world wish to see the Taliban model of dealing with women become the norm in the whole of Pakistan, Central Asia, Malaysia, Indonesia and other parts of the world where fundamentalism is allowed to establish itself?

The world of the 21st century cannot countenance the barbaric practices of earlier eras of human history where women were trampled under foot as a matter of course. It cannot remain a mute witness to institutionalised savagery on any segment of the population. In cases where it is undertaken as a policy sanctified by religious or any other dispensation of a similar nature it has to be fought by the global community as a whole. Inhuman practices from the dark ages enforced upon hapless citizens through brutality and terror demand that the perpetrators of these misdeeds on women and children be themselves brought to book. A distinguished writer had this to say on the subject:

> *"Please do not try to find points of contact with barbarism".*
>
> -India International Centre Quarterly, Spring 2000,

Instead of 'trying to find points of contact with barbarism' the answer would lie in demanding compliance with global norms for the treatment of women before any aid is dispensed in the Cauldron, regardless of drought, flooding, or other natural or man-made calamities. Aid would become conditional to educational institutions being set up for women with the help of global agencies in demarcated compounds. Aid sent to regimes of this nature first invariably fattens the tyrants and only leftovers are made available to the remainder.

This is not simply a matter concerning any given country where fanatical elements have seized power through violence. Whatever the initial justification, it ceases to have relevance where the medieval codes have to be continuously enforced through coercive action - with the greatest vehemence against women. If given the freedom to choose, the majority of the women under the Taliban dispensation would unhesitatingly be glad to remove the yoke.

Nuclear Proliferation

The other matter requiring urgent attention is the threat of nuclear proliferation. It is no longer a threat in being. Under the 'smoke screen' of threats to use nuclear weapons against India - an exercise in absurdity seeing India's size and ability to retaliate decisively - the real work of clandestine nuclear proliferation of suitcase bombs for use by bin Laden clones could be well under way. It is the latter nuclear threat that is crying for attention as it threatens the whole world. Delay in neutralising this threat at source would be unpardonable. While it could take decades for the major powers of the world to harmonise their working for safeguarding the planet as a whole, actions for limiting nuclear terrorism that cannot be postponed are listed below:

- Putting a *cordon sanitaire* around the A-P cauldron. The Russians have already begun to do so jointly with the Central Asian Republics. The United States has to coordinate with Russia to check this global menace. Geopolitical rivalries can be put on the backburner for the time being.
- China too will have to be co-opted to make the sanitisation effective.
- Similar cooperation will have to be effected between India and possibly the Gulf States.
- A global protocol, or Security Council declaration, on nuclear terrorism to the effect that: "wherever nuclear weapons are used by terrorists or nuclear blackmail effected through terrorism no country would be permitted to provide sanctuary to the terrorists and all concessions obtained under threat of nuclear terrorism would remain voided *post facto*".
- Additionally, the heads of government, armed forces and agencies backing terrorists using nuclear blackmail will be prosecuted for crimes against humanity and international warrants for their arrest

issued under the directions of the International Criminal Court.

- Russia and USA to put into immediate effect a joint over watch of the Cauldron. It should be made known that at the first sign of any nuclear-tipped missile taking off in any direction, or nuclear material leaving the Cauldron in any form, the two powers will be obliged to jointly neutralise all existing facilities capable of producing or launching such weapons. The riposte for nuclear blackmail would be similar. The onus for disproving the provenance of such weapons would lie with the authorities in the Cauldron.

- Russia, taking off from the strengthened defensive deployment in CAR, could make the declaration unilaterally, should the USA show hesitation to make a joint declaration. (Russia has to realise that the battle for Chechnya cannot be won in Chechnya. It will have to be fought in the A-P cauldron by means other than the deployment of ground forces).

The Subcontinental Response

The most important aspect which must be understood by the people of the subcontinent - and the world - is that the Kashmir question of the new century has little bearing with the problem that surfaced over fifty years ago. Too many externalities have been superimposed. These include:

Demographic swamping in areas occupied by Pakistan (modeled on the pattern perfected in Tibet and Xinjiang); the induction of foreign mercenaries and criminals; displacement forced on the population through terrorism; and declaration of *jehad* by quasi-independent religious groups who are in a position to challenge the authority of the state.

Put more succinctly: "the crisis facing the subcontinent and points north, west and east is no longer limited to the question of territorial adjustments. It has assumed the larger ideological dimension of *militant* Islam versus *liberal* Islam". The absence of any real democracy, proliferation of small arms, and easy access to drug money have all played their part in keeping the Cauldron on the boil. Up till now the brunt has been largely borne by India because Pakistan was able to convince the Western world that the problem related to Kashmir and nothing else. It took full fifty years for the rest of the world to come to the same conclusion as the Government of India, that Kashmir provided a convenient camouflage for the larger game plan. By the time the realisation came the elements pushing the fundamentalist creed had been immeasurably strengthened. When the West saw the light of day it was almost too late.

China meanwhile had its own strategy for the Great Game. It stepped in with a type of weapons support that made the earlier support given by the West pale into comparative insignificance. Whatever China's reasoning, by an unintended quirk of fate, a situation has been created that could actually help to ease India's burden in the longer term, provided the country continues to meet the terrorist challenge with unabated vigour and does not create greater strategic vulnerability in its northeast. This requires elaboration.

Regardless of all else Pakistan, while rattling the nuclear sabre, is well on the road to self-destruction. Not because of Indian action but because of the global reaction to a potential threat that could as easily manifest itself in the underbelly of Europe or an American city as it does in Chechnya. Viewed in that light - by providing the wherewithal to forces in the A-P cauldron who are inimical to global harmony - China emerges as a strong sustainer of global instability through the potential of nuclear terrorism. To date, it has been taken for granted that the targets of the *jehadis* are primarily in India, America, Central Asia and Russia. It is only a matter of time before several East Asian countries with mixed populations start feeling the heat. China's immediate neighbourhood too could become hot at several points.

It would be facile, and possibly tragic to call the struggle that will follow as a 'clash of civilisations'. It is certainly not the case. To give a civilisational veneer to the indoctrinated fanatics spilling out of the *madrasas* in the Cauldron or those who mastermind the terror would not only be a travesty of fact but a monumental error of judgment. Should the highly imaginative theory going by that name gain currency it could deal a body blow to Islam, not only in the Cauldron, in many other parts of the world as well.

India is perhaps the only country that can prevent that tragic outcome. Regardless of its differences with its hostile neighbour to its west it is home to nearly 130 million Muslims. They are Indian citizens. While some among them may have been subverted - in their hearts or minds - by the blandishments of the militants, the vast majority of them have contributed considerably to the progress that India has made since its independence.

Without saying so openly many Pakistanis, not wedded to militancy, do privately admit that India remains the only real bulwark against the terminal madness engulfing their state. Thus while the world puts into effect the tough measures to contain the menace within the Cauldron, India's efforts - besides toughening its stance against terrorism - should be directed towards strengthening liberal Islam in India and the subcontinent.

It is not simply a coincidence that for over fifty years the brunt of the menace of terrorism has been borne by the few million people of the beautiful Kashmir Valley. It continues to remain the focus of the *jehadis*. The reason has been alluded to earlier in the paper. The Valley, in a manner of speaking, was a shining example of the Sufi spirit in India. The militant beast comes not to ravish the beauty, but to destroy it. The tragic tale unfolds poignantly in the Akshara Theatre, New Delhi documentary, *The Kashmir Story* and docudrama, *The Sufi Way*. If the beauty perishes Kashmir perishes. Should the beauty remain the beast is slain.

Those at the helm of affairs in India have also to realise that Islam, although a transplant, helped to create one of the most magnificent Islamic heritages of the past thousand years. Beyond the killings and suppression of the adherents of the older Indian faiths lay the synthesis of a unique blend that led to a cultural efflorescence, the parallel to which would be difficult to find except in the European renaissance. Hence, an essential element of the fight against Islamic militants which India, the Central Asian Republics and other countries facing this threat may have been neglecting - by concentrating solely on the military dimension - is the need to strengthen liberal elements at the grass roots. India has to take the lead in preventing the *jehadisation* of Islam.

The vast majority of ordinary Muslims do not wish to see their religion degraded in this fashion. They have failed to organise themselves against the fanatical fringes in their respective countries, simply because the latter happen to have embraced terror. The excerpt that follows sums up the situation admirably:

> *"Yet, for all the cruelty and obscurantism associated with religion, hidden within the great traditions of faith are precious resources for the*

> *future welfare of humanity and these are too important to be abandoned to the extremists"*
>
> -Marcus Braybrooke, IIC Quarterly, Spring, 2000.

Extremism can only be established through extreme violence visited upon innocent, law-abiding people. Once established it can be perpetuated only through mindless savagery. Exactly what is being witnessed in Afghanistan; and that which is sought to be imposed on parts of Kashmir. But the world has just started emerging from one dark tunnel of this nature. Thirty years ago the experiment of extremism was tried out in Iran, although the case of Iran was very different. Nonetheless, after decades of suffering the people have had enough of the draconian enforcement codes. They have started mustering the courage to start protesting. They have a long road ahead.

Nobody, however, doubts that a moderate and tolerant regime, which is the natural state for any civilised society, will eventually be established in Iran. Do the people of Pakistan, who still haven't gone under as a country, wish to again enter the dark tunnel. The difference would be that this particular tunnel might have a blocked exit. The Iranians have started seeing the light. Iranian reformers have started openly accusing their government of past excesses:

> *"Your management of the judiciary in the past several months has not only created hopelessness among the people, but it is also leading to a future full of anxiety and apprehension".* {The Pro-reform Islamic Iran Participation Front (IIPF), in an open letter to the Judiciary. *(Times of India,* July 17, 2000)}

The people of Pakistan, mainly on account of apathy and inertia, are entering the region of darkness. India might no longer be interested in pulling them out at the other end. The words that follow have been spoken by a Pakistani:

> ".... perhaps does not realise that a sovereign Pakistan will go more swiftly to its doom than a Pakistan restrained by its external obligations".
>
> —Khaled Ahmed, Lahore based journalist, writing in *The Pioneer*, July 15, 2000.

Future Projections

The moderate leader of Iran, President Khatami, in a moment of eloquence, spoke of a 'Dialogue of the Civilisations'. It was widely reported in the world press after the interview to an American television chain. Wise words from a wise leader, aware of the difficulties that will have to be surmounted in mitigating the hardships to his people, resulting from past excesses. The even greater difficulty of prising loose from the vice-like grip of the self-anointed repositories of the ultimate wisdom, the draconian powers still wielded by them. The question is not only relevant for Islam but for the world that has achieved scientific breakthroughs of a type that could not have been even remotely guessed at by the founders of the great religions of the world.

Therefore, should the moderate and the liberal elements amongst the people of the region practicing Islam succeed in overcoming the obscurantist whose practice of the great religion begins and ends with the whip, the prospect for global harmony would be immensely strengthened.

Should the powers who are in a position to influence events in the Cauldron temporarily sink their differences to neutralise the menace emanating from it so that not even a residual strain remains, the world of the 21st century would start looking a different place. Were a condition of stability to prevail, the advantages that would accrue to almost every country are inconceivable at the present juncture.

First and foremost, like the days of yore, Marco Polo type of journeys along the Silk Route would be possible, to and fro, across the vast Central Asian expanse for people from the north, south, east and west. A family from Vietnam could plan to drive to Helsinki, a Chinese family to London, a Swedish family to Goa. The possibilities for easier travel across the Eurasian landmass are endless. The economic benefits unsurpassable. Fifty years down the road national boundaries would only be delineated on maps. The *kabuliwallah* of the subcontinental folklore of an earlier era would again roam freely in the bazaars of Bombay, Calcutta and even Shanghai. The Ladakhi would be able to cross Tibet in peace and reach Korea, if he wished to do so.

The Central Asian Republics could become a loose confederation along the lines of the European Union, sharing their oil and water for the benefit of the region as a whole. Pipelines could be laid from anywhere to anywhere, following alignments that were economically and ecologically the best options, bringing prosperity in their wake from the Caspian Sea to Colombo.

The 'Demilitarisation of the Himalayas as an Ecological Imperative' could commence within the next two to three years. The proposal put forward by the Ecology Monitors Society in November 1998 at an international conference held at New Delhi could then be progressed with greater confidence.

Each one of these aspects which might appear to be unachievable now takes on a different hue once the true measure of a demilitarised, 'de-fundamentalised' Cauldron are viewed from the perspective outlined above. By just excising the cancer from the Cauldron a dozen other trouble spots will subside. The vista which will then open out for Central and South Asia would be truly magnificent.

CONCLUDING REMARKS

Religion is being used as a tool for the most irreligious mayhem in the world. The problem will have to be dealt with globally at several levels. People who underestimate the potential of the menace being introduced into the global blood stream should recall how a mere handful of terrorists without the means of mass destruction available to them in the 1970s and 80s were able to create havoc in some of the most advanced societies in the world. In the present case the state itself becomes the master terrorist. Compared to that earlier period the evil being spawned now is several orders of magnitude more horrid than what went before. When the *jehadis* get hold of low yield suitcase nuclear devices - and it is only a matter of time before they do - the world will realise the folly of its inaction when the evil could have been nipped in the bud.

The Great Game is over. It has nearly gotten out of the hands of the powers that be. In the era of weapons of mass destruction almost all the big games are over. Only foolish people, die-hard diplomats from an earlier period, or the uniformed fraternity can really think of playing games on a global scale.

It is time to take stock.

(*Authors Note: Had the strategy outlined in the above presentation been adhered to the outcome could have been different. The opprobrium that the USA faces due to the savage bombing could conceivably have been avoided* to a large extent. In a nutshell, the strategy recommended, with sensible modifications to suit the actual conditions, called for putting into effect a 'cordon sanitaire'. Had the first action of the US forces been the positioning of forces and high-tech obstacle belts along the Afghan-Pakistan border - with heightened round the clock surveillance - to cut off the Taliban forces from their supply lines in Pakistan they could have been tackled in a far more efficacious manner. No matter how porous the border a fairly effective interdiction could have been planned 'prior' to commencement of hostilities. The period – lasting weeks or months - would have been utilized to squeeze in the Taliban from all sides and to assess the degree of cooperation being made available by the Pakistan military hierarchy and the ISI. Confidentiality as to the pattern of operations envisaged till the situation had clarified itself would have helped to retain surprise – both at the operational and tactical levels. Psywar operations should have commenced prior to the bombing assaults while a fairly large percentage of the Muslim population in Pakistan and elsewhere remained neutral after the September 11 outrage. A thought should have been given to raising Afghan UN Peacekeeping & Peace enforcement battalions from among the Afghan refugees after careful selection and training. This can still be put into effect for the next phase of post-intervention activities).

Journal of the United Service Institution of India, Vol CXXX, No. 541, July-September 2000.

End Notes

1. Dr. Ronald McCoy, Sandosham Memorial Lecture, 37th Annual Scientific Seminar, Malaysian Society of Parasitology & Tropical Medicine, 24 February 2001
2. Verse 40:7
3. Marcus Braybrooke, *India International Centre Quarterly*, Spring, 2000
4. *Indian Express*, `Musharraf Wants a Bangalore in Pakistan' by Rohit Darshan and Sudhan Kumar, August 19, 2001
5. `Nation undergoes slow torture', by Ayaz Amir, *The Times of India*, August 17, 2001
6. Singapore's Senior Minister, Mr. Lee Kuan Yew, in an interview published in *The Washington Times*. (Reproduced in *The Hindu*, May 20, 2001).
7. Brain Drain Worsens Chaos in Pakistan, Burhan Wazir, *The Observer*, London, July 1, 2001.
8. *The Hindu*, October 21, 2001,
9. Report of the Inter-Agency Needs Assessment Mission dispatched by the Secretary General of the United Nations to the Federal Republic of Yugoslavia.
10. India Fears Drug Glut From Afghanistan, by Shah Imran Ahmed, *Pioneer*, October 21, 2001.
11. Anthony Hyman. Afghanistan Under Soviet Domination: 'The Land and the People in History', 1984, pp 5-6.

MAP OF AFGHANISTAN AND NEIGHBOURING COUNTRIES

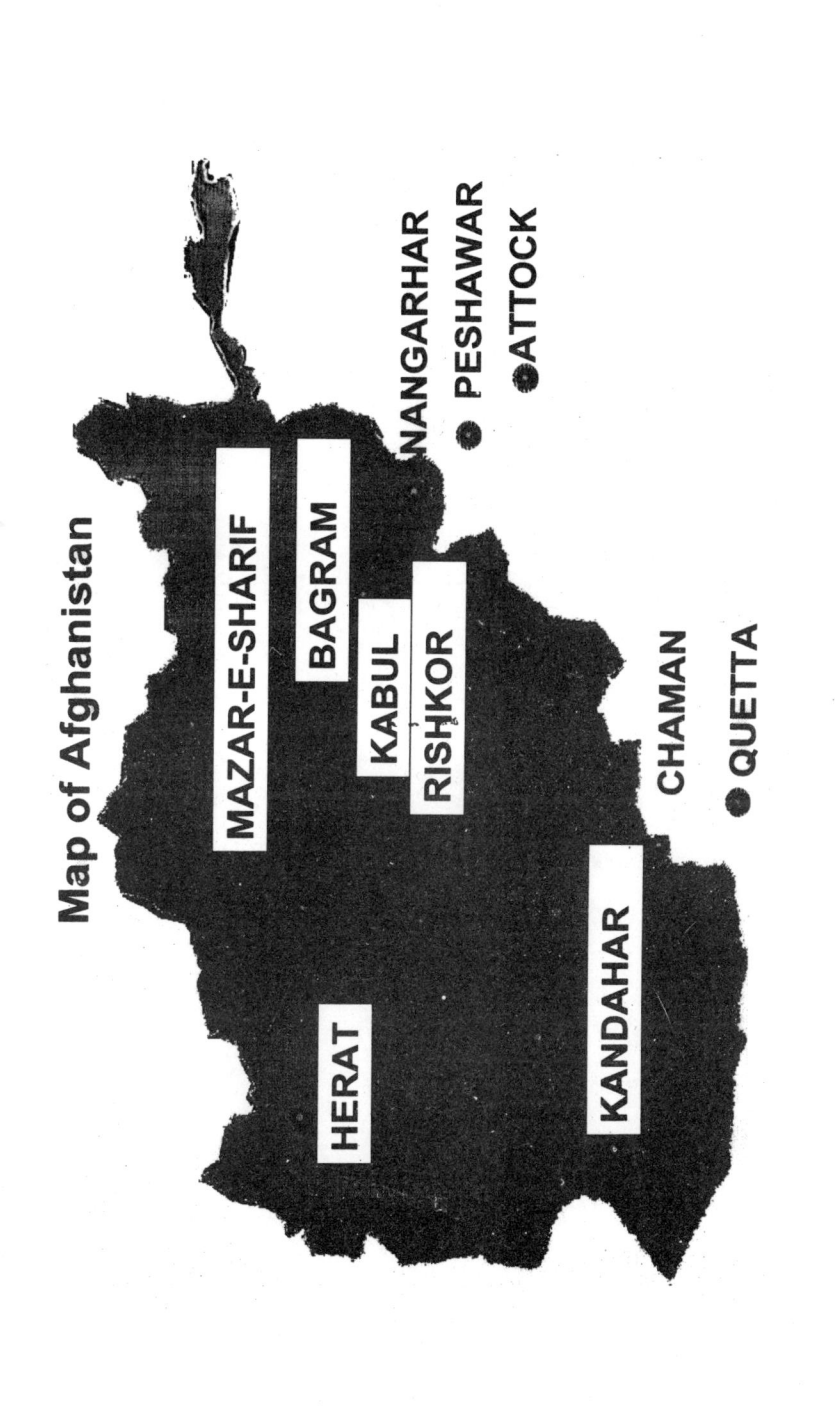

Map of Afghanistan

MAZAR-E-SHARIF
BAGRAM
NANGARHAR
• PESHAWAR
• ATTOCK
KABUL
RISHKOR
HERAT
CHAMAN
• QUETTA
KANDAHAR

Index

ABM Treaty, 211
Afghan People, 121, 123, 124, 125, 161
Afghan Refugee, 87, 134
Afghan Regime, 76
Afghan Scene, 183
Afghan Society, 81, 173, 174
Afghan UN Peace-keeping & Peace Enforcement, 228
Afghan, 168, 180, 182
Afghanistan and Central Asia, 98
Afghanistan Pakistan Fundamentalism, 214
Afghanistan, 172
Afghanistan, Talibanisation, 15, 39
Afghanistan, 6, 17, 20, 21, 23, 27, 39, 41, 42, 49, 50, 55, 56, 60, 65, 66, 67, 68, 71, 76, 77, 82, 88, 89, 91, 95, 96, 107, 107, 108, 110, 112, 114-116,118, 121, 123, 125, 126, 128, 129, 130, 132-135, 138, 140, 147,148,150-154, 156, 158, 161, 169, 170, 173, 174, 179, 180, 182, 183, 184, 187, 191, 192, 194, 195, 196-201, 203, 206, 207, 208, 215, 224
   Central and Western-, 124
   Civil War in-, 149, 172
   Military, 134, 188
   Muslims in, 146
   Northern, 148
   Northern,Central and Western, 197
   Operations in-,199
   Refugees, 117
   Soviet in, 107
   Taliban, 119
   War, 150
   Women of, 209, 210
Afghanistan-Pakistan Axis, 208
Afghanistan-Pakistan Cauldron, 206, 208, 210, 211, 21, 215, 218, 219
Afghanistan-Pakistan Cell, 220, 221, 222, 225, 227
Afghans, 157, 159
Agra Summit, 83
Ahmed Shah Masood, 183, 184
Al Qaeda, 41, 44, 112, 113, 114, 154, 155, 156, 183, 187, 194, 200
Algeria, 172
America, 6, 7, 16, 30, 32, 40, 44, 57, 83, 92, 107, 110, 111, 114, 115, 119, 131, 132, 136, 137, 139,143, 148, 151, 153, 155, 156, 159, 160, 163, 164, 174, 175, 181, 182, 191, 195, 198, 199, 200,203, 209, 212, 221, 222, 225
American Economy, 189
American Geo-Strategic Interest,142
American Imperialism, 182
AmericanUltimatum, 89, 90
Amu Darya, 149
Anglo-American Forces, 164
Anglo-American Intervention, 135
Anglo-American Media, 164, 183
Anglo-American Military, 196
Anglo-American, 180

Anglo-US Interest, 127
Anglo-US Military 142
Anti-Social Activities, 28
Arab World, 83, 89, 137, 140, 170, 182, 216
Arabia, 30
Arabian Peninsula, 43, 44, 143, 144
Arabian Sea, 134, 193
Arabs, 29, 31, 145
Army, 47, 79,111
Asia and Africa, 217
Asia and Eurasia,108
Asia (ns), 7, 68, 108, 127, 163
Asian Societies, 174,
Atlantic and Pacific Oceans, 164
Autocracy and Theocracy, 21
Autonomy, 48, 97
Ayatholla Khomeini, 56, 143
Ayub Khan (FM), 48, 80

BCCI, 63
Bahrain, 172
Baluchi, 27
Baluchinstan, 9, 51, 116
Baluchistan and Sindh, 64, 67
Bangladesh, 21, 29, 30, 49, 51, 146, 171.177, 210
Bank of England, 6
Barbaric Regimes, 20
Begran, 125
Beijing, 179
Berlin Wall, 56
Bhutan and India, 102
Bhutto, Benazir, 16
Bhutto,Z.A, 73, 90
Bihar and U.P., 29
Black Money, 61
Bombay,Calcutta and Shanghai, 226
Britain, 160, 164
British Empire, 43,
British Indian Empire, 75

British, 18, 23, 45, 49, 127, 128, 155, 160, 170, 172
Brunei, 45
Bush,W.George, 137, 147, 164, 189
Bush (Senior), 183
Cavern Defences, 156
Central and South Asia,125, 226
Central Asia, 23, 27, 30, 68, 69, 91, 92, 108, 113, 125, 128, 129, 134-135, 147-149, 153, 154, 155, 173, 179, 185, 187,196, 201, 217, 222,
Central Asian Countries, 159
Central Asian Republics, 65, 68, 108, 123, 129, 212, 219, 223, 222
Chandigarh, 125
Chechnya, 215, 220, 221
China, 6, 7, 16, 19, 30, 49, 65, 68, 76, 88-90, 95, 104, 102, 105, 110, 111, 129, 131, 134, 135, 153, 172, 178, 179, 183, 185, 187, 196, 210, 211, 214, 219, 221, 222
Chinese Training Centres, 179
Chinese, 30, 105, 110, 172, 180, 210, 211, 217
Christian, 19, 146, 16
Christianity, 35
CIA, 60, 131, 151, 154, 155
Civil Codes, 122
Civil Services, 70
Civil War, 47, 80,
Civilian Bureaucracy, 47
Civilisation, 19, 32, 54, 73, 117, 163, 167, 168, 222
Cold War, 7, 24, 60, 127, 137, 142, 150, 152, 158, 185, 188, 189, 191, 213
Colombo to Kabul, 49, 160
Colonalism, 92
Colonial Masters, 22
Colonial Power, 27, 160
Communication, 18, 110, 175,

Index

Communism, 7,
Constituent Assembly, 123
Corrupt Bureaucracy, 51
Corruption, 62
Counter Terrorism, 170
Criminalisation of Politics, 62
Cross Border Terrorism, 68, 77
Cultural and Economic Exchanges, 93

Dalai Lama, 26
David and Goliath, 151
De Gaulle, 80, 81
Defence Line, 130
Defence Outlay, 145
Demilitarisation of Himalayas, 98, 102, 226
Demilitarization of Sino-Indian Border, 105
Denuclearisation and Demilitarization of Tibet, 105
Destructive Weapons System, 102
Developing Countries, 42, 50, 55
Dictatorship, 47
Diplomacy, 127
Dress Codes, 9
Drug Trafficking, 50, 150
Durand Line, 125, 174

East Asian Countries, 222
East Pakistan (Bangladesh), 57
Eco Monitoring Society, 98, 102, 106, 157, 225
Eco Revival Plan, 103
Ecological Devastation, 98, 157
Economic Trade Agreement, 94
Eco-Restoration, 103, 105
Eco-Revival Summit, 102
Education, 27, 29, 30, 34, 44, 49, 87, 93,100, 114, 118, 121, 167, 168, 194
   Egypt, 140, 141, 145, 172
Elections, 61, 66, 71, 73
England and France, 43

Ethnic Cleansing, 215
Eurasian, 16, 35, 89, 128, 146, 157 175, 212, 226,
European Union, 137, 138, 226
European, 43, 127, 133, 141, 164, 223
Explosive Materials, 156
Extortionist, 51
Extremists, 37, 224

Family Planning, 87
FBI, 157
Ferghana Valley, 129
Festivals, 20, 21
First and Second World War, 138
Flora and Fauna, 157
Foreign Mercenaries, 220
Foreign Policy, 150
France, 80, 216
French Revolution, 216
Flesh Trade, 31, 61
Fundamantalism, 148, 214, 215, 217, 221
   Hindu, 49
Fundamentalism (ist), 16, 17, 19, 20, 28, 29, 49, 61, 70
Fundamentalist Islam, 214

Galileo, 35
Gandhi, Mahatma, 26
Gandhi,Indira, 73
Gandhi,Rajiv, 73
Gaza Strip, 146
Genetic Modificatons , 157
Genocide and Fratricide, 32
Geopolitical Imbalances, 217
Gilgit and Baluchistan, 68
Global Muslim Brotherhood, 29
Global Oil Reserve, 215
Global Community, 47, 48
Global Economic Recession, 188
Global Economy, 79
Global Terrorism, 6, 165
Global Warming, 49

Globalisation, 19, 24, 76, 79
Goa, 226
Golan Heights, 145
Golden Crescent, 150
Gorkha Pensioners, 106
Great Britain, 207
Greater Kabul, 125
Greek Thinkers and Philosophers, 35
Gulf, 134
Gulf States, 30, 138, 141, 142, 143, 144, 219
Gulf War, 137, 141, 142, 153, 166, 199
Gun Culture, 51, 52

Harrappan, 23
Haryana and Punjab, 125
Herat, 18
Helm, Richard, 131
Helsinki, 226
High Tech. Weapons, 199
Himalayas, 94, 102, 103
Hindu Population, 146
Hindukush, 124, 134, 149, 173
Hindus and Muslims, 48
Hosni Mubarak, 140, 141
Human Rights, 34, 178
Hydrocarbon Reserve, 128, 150

Illegal Migration, 117
Immigrant Communist, 53
Imperial Guard, 143
India (ns), 6, 15-19, 22, 27-30, 39, 40, 48, 49, 55, 56, 57, 60, 64, 65, 67, 69, 71, 73, 74, 77, 78, 79, 89, 91, 92, 94-96, 102, 103, 105, 124, 125, 127, 130, 131, 134, 135, 136, 143, 146, 149, 154, 158, 159, 160, 171, 172, 173, 179, 193, 196, 212, 213, 216, 217, 219, 221, 222, 223, 224
    Afghan Policy, 160
    Ancient Culture, 59

Community in Fiji, 146
Democracy, 49, 73
Economic strength, 67
Electorate, 49
Leavers, 60, 65
North India, 173
War Against -, 60, 95
War With, 22,
India and Pakistan, 75, 88, 93, 94, 98, 99, 100
    Political Hindus, 88
    Prime Ministers of-, 104
India International Centre, 98, 102
India-China Sector, 103, 104
Indian Ocean, 139
Indian –Pakistan Section, 103
Indo Pak Economic Commission, 94
Indo Pakistan Brigade, 99
Indo-Afghan Relations, 158
Indonesia, 29, 170, 215, 216, 217
Indo-Pak Dispute Setlement Tribunal, 99
Indo-Pak Scientific Teams, 104
Indo-Pakistan Relations, 91, 96, 97
Indo-US Relations, 68
Industrialised World, 144
Information Technology, 55
Internal Criminal Court, 220
International Court of Justice (Hague), 100, 104, 105
International Court, 213
International Criminal Court, 212
International Law, 215
Interpol, 212
Iran and Russia, 153
Iran Revolution, 20
Iran, 20, 56, 65, 87, 113, 123, 124, 126, 130-134, 142, 143, 148, 153, 172, 179, 196, 201, 224,
Iran's Afghan Policy, 134
Iranian Armed Forces, 131, 132
Iranian Military, 142
Iranian Monarchy, 143
Iranian Reforms, 224

Index

Iranians, 133, 135, 159
Iran-Iraq War, 133, 152, 166
Iraq, 133, 134, 137, 141, 142, 143, 172
Iraqi, 153
Iraqi Economy, 152
Irrigation Channel Schemes, 122
ISI Funds, 28
ISI, 57, 60, 72, 81, 110, 111, 119, 154, 155, 174, 189, 181, 193, 228
Islam, 7, 19, 22, 25, 26, 33, 36, 38, 39, 40, 42, 48, 59, 57, 80, 83, 101, 108, 109, 129, 136, 139, 141, 165, 166, 167, 182, 216, 222, 223,
Radical, 42, 47,48, 50, 55, 57, 63, 65, 66, 71
Islamabad, 48, 76, 98, 116, 179, 198, 214,
Islamic Population, 215
  (Malaya, Indonesia, Phillipines, Bangladesh, Myanmar, Central Asia, Middle East,)
Islamic, 6, 7, 15, 19, 21, 24, 26, 37, 50, 56, 59, 67, 68, 71, 118, 128, 129, 130, 138, 139, 146, 168, 176, 177, 223,
  Countries, 59
  Culture, 59
  Faith, 40
  Fundamentalism, 146,148
  Jehad, 41, 91, 118
  Law, 29
  Purity, 50
  Radical, 44
  Radical Group, 57, 66, 67, 69, 71, 90, 146
  Societies, 33
  State, 117
  World, 41, 44
Islamic Bomb, 63, 83
Islamic Centres, 127, 128
Islamic Doctrines, 35

Islamic Fundamentalism (ist), 81, 82, 134, 141, 194
Islamic Nations, 135
Islamic Radicalism, 87, 127
Islamic Regime, 209
Islamic Resurgence, 133
Islamic Union, 138
Islamisation, 64, 69, 70
Islamist Forces, 139
Islamist Terrorist, 151
Islamist Groups, 80
Israel, 44, 141, 145, 146, 172,

Jamait-Ulema-Islam, 203
Jammu & Kashmir Sector, 103
Jammu and Kashmir, 68, 94, 97, 103
Japan, 126, 142, 146
Jehad(i), 16, 23, 26, 40, 41, 43, 50, 55, 57, 70, 72, 77, 87, 97, 170, 171, 172, 182, 187, 208, 210 211, 213, 216, 220, 222, 223, 227
Jehad Against India,203
Jehadisation, 194
Jinnah, (Mohd.Ali), 26, 27, 209
Jodhpur, 27
Jordon, 145, 172
Jordon Royal Family, 145
Junagarh, 27

Kabul and Colombo, 91
Kabul, 17, 18, 125, 160, 174, 179, 182, 194, 199
Kandhar, 18
Kangaroo Court, 216
Karachi, 54, 67, 76
Kargil Debacle, 208
Kargil Misadventure, 57, 88
Kashmir Valley, 21, 22, 214, 223,
Kashmir, 39, 40, 57, 68, 77, 78, 88, 92, 96, 94, 95, 97, 112, 113, 220, 221, 214, 215, 224
Kashmiriyat, 214
Kemal Ataturk, 80, 81, 138, 167

Kemalian Role, 138
Khatami (President), 225
Khomeini Revolution, 20, 143, 163, 166
King, Martin Luther, 26
Korea, 226
Kosovo Affairs, 199
Kuwait, 142, 152, 172,

Labour Party (UK), 151
Ladakh, 226
Ladakh Sector, 103
Laden, 181- 183, 187 (See under Osama)
Lahore Process, 88
Land Rights, 122
Language Ethnicity, 31
Law Courts, 216
Lebanon, 145, 172
Lee Kuan Yew, 82
Legislation,35, 100
Lenin, 143
Lethal Weapons, 201
Libya and Saudi Arabis, 63
Lion of Panjshir, 129, 183
LOC, 94, 97
London, 76, 117, 179, 226
Longer Range Missile, 179

Marco Polo, 226
Madarasa 27, 28, 65, 66, 114, 117, 149, 177, 182, 200, 212 ,215 ,222
Maffias and Radical Islamic Group, 62
Malaysia, 217
Masonic Lodge, 31
Masood, Ahmed Shah, 129, 131, 132, 142, 143
Massacre, 22
Mazar-I-Sharif, 198
Media, 57, 72, 189
Medieval Islamic Codes, 100
Medieval System, 20
Medieval Theocracy, 178

Mediterrainian, 139, 141
Meiji Japan, 168
Mercenaries, 37
Middle Ages, 28, 167
Middle East, 30, 43, 65, 147, 159, 166
Migrations, 171, 172
Militancy, 37, 69
Militant Group, 58, 72
Militant Islamic Group, 60, 95, 141
Military Bases, 42
Military Bureaucracy, 48
Military Dictatorship, 59, 75
Military Hierarchy, 57, 63
Military Industry,. 29
Military Rule, 216
Military, 6, 7, 16, 24, 49, 57, 58-67, 69, 70, 71, 72, 75-77, 79-81, 88, 93, 99, 102, 105, 108, 110, 113, 118, 119, 134, 141, 143, 144, 147, 149, 153, 158, 170, 174, 181, 186, 187, 192, 196, 199, 200,201, 207, 210, 213, 216, 217, 222
   Activities, 105
   Bosses, 116
   Coups, 76, 109, 174
   Dictator, 80, 90
   Equipments, 142
   Exchanges, 98
   Expenditure, 88
   Forces, 102
   Generals, 81
   Hierarchy, 96, 109
   Operations, 105, 112, 188
   Pakistan, 82, 91, 96
   Regime, 58, 130, 213
   Resources, 129
   Rulers, 116
   Security Horizon, 77
   Strategies, 147
Military-Jehadi, 64
Mirza, Iskandar, 48

Index

Missile Technology(ies), 68, 95
Moghul Rule, 23
Mohammad, 23
Moscow, 148
Mossadaq, 131
Mother Teresa, 26
MQM, 67
Mujahideen, 60, 107, 150
Muscle/Money Power, 61
Muslim Clergy, 8
Muslim Fundamentalist, 146, 211
Muslim Nuclear Weapon, 82
Muslim Rulers, 187
Muslim Societies, 181, 182
Muslim World, 166, 169, 181, 183, 187, 195
Muslim(s), 23, 25, 27, 28, 29, 30-33, 38, 40, 42, 44, 45, 80, 82, 112, 119, 138, 139, 146, 140, 150, 159, 163, 166, 167, 168, 170, 171, 172, 175, 180, 222, 223, 228
  Brotherhood, 30, 31
  Chinese, 30
  Clergy, 29, 30, 31, 59, 108
  Countries, 24
  Indian-, 30
  Majority, 27
  Pakistani-, 30
  Radical-Group, 113
  Religion, 27
  Rule, 27
  Society, 34, 36, 139
  Ummah, 29
  World, 138, 139
  Women, 31

Narcotic Traffic, 159
Narco-Crime Syndicate, 70
Narcotic Network, 88
Narcotic Trafficking, 129
Narcotics, 63, 150, 179, 612
  Mafias, 63
Narco-Trafficking, 31

Nasser of Egypt, 140, 183
Nasser's Pan Arabism, 140
National Missile Defence (NMD), 132, 165, 186, 189
National Security, 158
Nawaz Sharif, 88
Nazi Germany, 211
Nepal, 102
Nepalese, 102
New Delhi, 74, 97, 98, 116, 160, 223, 226
Non-Muslim Minorities, 176
Non-Punjabi Generals, 111,
Non-Pushtun, 134
Non-Resident Indians, 98
Non-Western Nuclear Power, 185
Northern Alliance, 120, 124, 129, 130, 133, 134, 148, 153, 159, 181, 184, 182, 187, 195, 197, 198, 199
Northern Areas (Gilgit, Baluchistan), 214
Nuclear Arsenal and Delivery System, 153
Nuclear Black Mail, 56, 60, 219, 220
Nuclear Exchange, 185
Nuclear Materials, 220
Nuclear Missile High-tech., 153
Nuclear Sabre, 221
Nuclear Terrorism, 219, 222
Nuclear Tipped Missile, 220
Nuclear War Against India, 210
Nuclear War, 207
Nuclear Weapons, 43, 141, 53, 63, 83
Nuclear, 63, 217, 227
  Development
  Infrastructure, 63
  Material, 63, 68
  Powers, 105
  Programme, 63
Nuclear/WMD, 165
NWFP and Baluchistan, 111

NWFP, 51, 60, 96, 116, 125

Oil Revenue, 45
Oman, 172
Omar, 183
OPEC, 142, 144, 145
Opium-Poppy Crop, 159
Organisation of Islamic Conference,(OIC), 45
Orthodox Clergy, 33
Osama, 55, 81, 83, 107, 111, 112, 114, 136, 143-145, 183, 191, 194, 195, 197, 213
Osama, Bin Laden, 151, 154, 155, 156, 203, 212, 215
Ottoman Empire, 138, 167

Pacific Ocean, 68
Pak Afghan Hinterland, 187
Pakhtoonistan, 194
Pakistan and Bangladesh, 61
Pakistan India, 89
Pakistan Saudi Arabian, 134,
Pakistan Saudi Nexus, 136
Pakistan, 6-8, 15-18, 20-22, 24, 26, 27, 29, 30, 36, 37, 39, 40, 42, 43, 47-56, 58-61, 63, 65-71, 72, 74, 76, 77, 78, 79, 80, 83, 87-93, 94, 95, 96, 98, 102, 103, 107, 108, 109, 110, 111, 112, 115-119, 123, 124, 127, 128, 129, 130, 132, 137, 147-154, 156, 159,-161, 167, 170, 172, 173, 174, 177179, 181, 182, 186, 193-198, 206, 208, 209, 213, 216, 217, 220, 221, 222, 224, 228
   Army, 112, 210
   Break up of , 65
   Citizens of , 100, 118
   Constitution, 75
   Defence Expenditure, 50
   Democracy, 75
   Dictator, 80, 90

Economic Cooperation with India, 114
Economic Rehabilitation, 193
Economy of, 61, 113, 154
Ethnic Grouping, 119
Fundamentalism in , 208
General HQ., 187
Generals, 56, 81, 116
Ghattoisation, 117
Jehadi Elements, 55, 56, 77
Jehadisation of, 60, 63
Kashmir Policy of, 97
Military, 50, 55, 56, 60, 62, 64, 66, 81, 108, 110, 117, 151, 154,174, 179, 187, 124, 193-195, 197, 208, 210, 211, 228
Military Forces, 117
Military Government of , 78, 92
Military Head of, 107
Military Hierarchy, 50, 63
Military Intelligence Service in, 69
Military Leaders of , 49, 117
Military Regimes-, 61, 115
Muslims in, 146, 216
Nuclear Arsenal of , 179, 208
Nuclear Capability, 112
Nuclearisatioin of, 208
Political Process in, 116
Population, 54, 55
Pushtuns, 117
Radicalisation of , 77
Rulers, 79, 81
Security, 77
Society, 50, 60, 64, 177, 180, 194,209
Talibanisation of, 194
Truncation of, 125

Index

War Machines, 69
Pakistan-Afghanistan Refugee, 115
Pakistan-Afghanistan Sector, 103
Palestinian Problem, 166
Palestinian Question, 146, 147
Palestinian, 145
Pan Islamic, 83, 92, 207
Pan-Islamism, 133
PARSA, 209
Partition, 94
Pax-Americana, 155
Pax-Britannica, 155
Pearl Harbour, 185
Pentagon Attacks, 132, 180, 185, 187
Persian Gulf, 142, 143
Persian, 131
Plebiscite, 214
Political and Economic Dominance, 33
Political Parties, 47, 51, 57, 59, 61, 66
Politico-Religious Orthodoxy, 169
Post Gulf War, 153
Post Taliban, 148
Post World War, 127, 160
Post-Colonial Era, 75, 128, 139
Post-Taliban, 180
Poverty Alleviation, 100
Prophet, 176, 177 (see Mohammed also)
Prostitution, 126
Provincial Autonomy, 75
Punjab, 69, 74
Pushtuns, 19, 125, 159, 174,
Qatar, 172

Racial Attacks, 175
Radical Islamists, 32, 39, 42, 55, 56, 57, 58, 64, 66, 114,159
Radical Military, 33
Radicalism, 17, 19
Ranjit Singh (Maharaja), 173
Rawalpindi, 206

Red Cross, 126
Referendum, 124
Refugee Camps, 126, 127
Refugees, 195
Rehabilitation Programme, 122
Religion, 16, 17, 18, 27, 29, 31, 32, 36, 39, 40, 43, 49, 166, 172, 223, 225, 227
Religious Fundamentalist, 207, 212, 214
Religious Leaders, 26
Religious Orthodoxy, 28
Renaissance, 35
Rituals, 25
Robespierre, 216
Rohullah Khomeini, 132
Royal Nepalese Government, 105
Russia (n), 8, 30, 124, 128, 129, 130, 134, 135, 137, 143, 147, 148, 149, 153, 159, 160, 174, 179, 183, 193, 195, 196-197, 201, 212, 219, 220, 222
Russia and China, 201
Russia and USA, 212
Russia, China, and India, 133
Russian Republics, 130

Saddam Hussein, 137, 141, 143, 152, 183
Saigon, 565
Saudi Arabi, 27, 30, 63, 107, 108, 119, 127, 135, 136, 137, 141, 142, 143, 144, 148-151, 167, 172, 180, 193, 210
Saudi Monarchy, 143
Saudi Royal Family, 136, 143, 144
Saudi Rulers, 14
Saudi, 145
Saudis, 29
SAVAK, 131,
Science and Technology, 31, 34
Second .World War, 80
Sectarianism, 50
Security Council, 105, 200, 219,

Security, 53, 71, 72, 76, 172, 179, 192
Shanghai Cooperative Org., 129
Shanghai Group, 129
Shari'ah as Zimmis, 176, 178
Shia Group, 134
Siachin,103, 104
Silk Route, 226
Sinai Heights, 124
Sindhi, 27
Sino-Indian Border, 105
Slavery, 28, 33
Small Arms, 51-54, 88, 221
Social and Political Changes, 35
Social Movements, 29
Social Sector, 50
Society (ies), 17, 19, 26, 28, 29, 31, 33, 34, 36, 41, 50, 52, 53, 54, 60, 73, 88, 115, 139, 168, 169, 175, 178, 224, 22
    Civilized, 36, 37
    Democratic, 34
    Modern, 36
    Muslim, 25
    South Asian, 28
Socio-Economic Advancement, 28, 77
Socio-Political System, 75
South Asia, 24, 30, 49, 50, 83, 91, 98, 163, 174-176, 179
South East Asia, 172,
Soviet (Union), 6, 76, 78, 82, 88, 116, 118, 119, 128, 147, 148, 149, 150, 151, 159, 160, 172, 174, 210
Soviet Agression, 91,
Soviet and Americans, 107
Soviet Empire, 43, 60
Soviet Era, 139
Soviet Forces, 60, 148
Soviet Occupation in Afghanistan, 136
Special Security Council Resolution, 123

Srinagar, 21
State Security ,47
Stinger Missile, 150
Sub-Himalayan and Trans-Himalayan Region, 106
Sudan, 172 .
Saudi Oil, 144
Saudi, 142
Suffis, 23, 223
Sufi Mysticism, 214
Sufism, 39
Suicide Bombers, 34
Suicide Missions, 37, 43, 172, 188
Supreme Court, 99
Swedish Family,226
Syria, 145, 172

Taiwan and Tibet, 180
Tajikistan, 129
Taliban and Pakistani Training Camps, 87
Taliban, 16, 21, 29, 55, 56, 60, 65, 67, 76, 82, 86, 96, 110, 111, 114, 119, 128-130, 134, 135 , 148, 150, 151, 153, 154, 155, 157, 159, 160, 177, 178, 179, 180, 181, 182, 183,187, 188, 191, 193, 194, 195, 197, 200, 201, 208, 210, 217, 218,
Talibanisation, 40, 47, 114, 210
Talibanisation of Kashmir, 39 208, 210, 217, 218,
Tashkent, 179
Taxation Pattern, 122
Tehran and Isfahan, 131
Tehran, 134
Terrorism, 15, 32, 50, 53, 113, 117, 128, 129, 147, 151, 165, 179, 180, 183, 191, 194, 200, 201, 207, 211, 219, 222, 223
Terrorist Act, 110
Terrorist Attack, 53, 186
Terrorist Cell, 114
Terrorist Trade, 59

Index

Terrorist Training Camps, 150
Terrorist, 34, 42, 44, 128, 135, 141, 146, 151, 215, 219, 221, 227,
Theology, 36
Third World, 51
Tiananmen Squre Massacre, 6
Tibet and Xinjiang, 220
Tibet, 105, 226
Tibetans, 103
Tourism, 78, 94
Trade Route, 149
Tribal Areas, 51
Tribal, 198, 121
Tripoli to Oman, 140
Troop Reduction, 97
Turkey, 80, 138, 141, 167
Turkish Model, 140
Twin Towers, 40, 200
Tyson, Mike, 151

U Thant, 140
U.K. 127, 128, 131, 170
Uighur Separatist, 179
UN Committee, 157
UN Peace Keeping Operations, 99
UN Resolutions, 214
UN Sanctions, 137
United Arab Emirates, 172
United Arab Republic, 140
United Nations (UN), 120, 121, 12, 123, 124, 125, 146
United Nations Emergency Force, 140
United Nations, 150, 169, 186, 188
Uranium, 156
Urumchi and Kabul, 179
USA, 7, 32, , 40-42, 44, 45, 55, 60, 62, 66, 68, 76, 82, 83, 87 56, 88, 89, 90, 96, 97, 107, 108, 110, 111, 112, 113, 115, 116-120, 123, 127, 128, 130, 131, 132-137, 138, 140, 141, 142, 143, 146-153, 155, 157, 163, 164, 165, 168-170, 172, 173, 179-183, 185-200, 203, 210, 211, 212, 215, 219, 220, 228
Afghan Refugees, 228
Army, 152
Bombings, 169, 181, 182
Central Command, 193, 198
Citizens, 191, 192
Citizenship, 170, 191
Decision Making, 191
Economy, 142, 152
Entrepreneurs, 55
Forces, 192, 193, 228
Intelligence, 150
Military, 193, 194, 197, 200, 201
Military Aircraft, 150
Military Operations, 193
Military Strategies, 192
Military Wisdom, 189
Oil Interest, 153
Policy, 127, 128, 183, 191, 193
Politics, 164
Retaliation, 169, 181
Security, 164
Society, 187, 191
Taliban, 228
Taliban Forces, 228
Troops, 189
USSR, 56, 88, 89, 92, 95, 149, 207
Uzbekistan, 192, 196
Uzbek Warlord, 199
Uzbekistan, 134, 148
Veto Powers, 105
Vietnam, War, 191
Vietnam, 192, 226
Vindhyas, 54
Violence, 21, 26, 27, 50, 51, 53, 54, 62, 67, 70, 72, 166, 177, 224
Warlordism, 52

Washington, 116, 179, 188, 198, 203
Weapons of Mass Destruction, 43
Weapons, 53, 62, 122, 132, 172, 201, 220, 221, 227
West Bank, 146
Western Alliance, 30, 142, 143, 152, 153, 164, 187
Western Consortia, 126
Western Industries, 29
Western Power, 24
Western World, 127, 131, 133, 144, 146, 175, 186, 187, 221
Women Emancipation, 28, 114, 121
Women Empowerment, 28
World Bank, 105
World Economy, 144
World Order, 53
World War(s), 131, 171, 213
WTC(World Trade Centre), 40, 41, 45, 90, 94, 132, 165-169, 180, 185, 187
Xinjiang, 30, 179, 215
Yeltsin, 147
Yugoslavia, 157, 199
Zahir Shah, (King), 120
Zia-ul-Haq, 36, 55, 80, 107, 117 154, 194, 213